Contemporary Tangential Surrealist Poetry: An Anthology

Edited by Tony Kitt

SurVision Books

First published in 2023 by
SurVision Books
Dublin, Ireland
www.survisionmagazine.com

Introduction © Tony Kitt, 2023
The poems © their individual authors, 2023
This collection copyright © SurVision Books, 2023

Cover image: "Endless Flight" by Harue Koga, 1930
Design © SurVision Books, 2020

ISBN: 978-1-912963-44-7

This book is in copyright. No part of this publication may be reproduced, stored in a retrieval system or transmitted in any form or by any means without the prior permission in writing from the publisher.

CONTENTS

Tangential Surrealism by Tony Kitt	9
Will Alexander (USA)	
Steaming Silicate Fragmentation	13
Texas Blind Salamander Feelings	14
Somnolent Exhumation as Canticle	16
John Thomas Allen (USA)	
Dust	17
Roswell Construction	18
The Lighthouse above the Graveyard	19
Lee Ballentine (USA)	
Solecipsism	20
The Dead Body and the Living Body	21
The Fou-Gou	23
Clayre Benzadón (USA)	
Ephemera	25
Honeydew	27
Wheatfield Treehouse	28
Charles Borkhuis (USA)	
Face the Music and Dance	30
Further Instructions	32
Witness	34
Lily Brown (USA)	
Socket	36
Leaf at the End	37
Its Character	38
Garrett Caples (USA)	
Sundial Tone	40
André Breton's Apartment	41
Ordinary History America	43
Angela Cleland (Scotland)	
Cross	44
Looking back on it	45
Woodpigeon	46

Andrei Codrescu (USA)
    The Best Side of Me   48
    Bicycle   49
    Truth & Ruffles   50
Alison Dunhill (England)
    Ice Moon   51
    Cloud Construction   52
    Fountain   53
John Godfrey (USA)
    Pink Tab   54
    Light Years Ago   55
    Can You Tell   57
Philip Hammial (Australia)
    Ps & Qs   58
    Plateresque   59
    Tabloid   60
Roberto Harrison (USA)
    nocturnal heritage   61
    eat white   62
    dearest animal   64
Nicholas Alexander Hayes (USA)
    Ghost Lineage   65
    Root to Nourish Love   66
    Panspermia   67
Stefania Heim (USA)
    A Large Mirror Unloaded From a Truck in the Sun   68
    From "HOUR BOOK": 3:49PM   69
    From "HOUR BOOK": 6:35PM   70
Bob Heman (USA)
    The Story Of   71
    The Distance   72
    One Becomes   73
Helen Ivory (England)
    The Square of the Clockmaker   74
    Sister   75
    The Art Gallery   76

Andrew Joron (USA)
    Oedipus-Mask of an American Inventor   77
    Assumption, The   79
    Boreal   80
George Kalamaras (USA)
    The Fourth Way In   82
    The Sorrow of Listening   83
    This Roundness of Now   84
Charles Kell (USA)
    Asp   85
    Dead Letter Office   86
    Ambergris   87
Robert Kelly (USA)
    A Lithuanian Elegy   88
    Dream Debris   89
    A Woman with Flaxen Hair in Norfolk Heard   90
Tony Kitt (Ireland)
    A Collage Has a Thousand Mouths   91
    Twenty-Four Heavenly Snippets   92
    To My Real/Imaginary Daughter   93
Noelle Kocot (USA)
    Ascent of the Mothers   94
    The Moon   95
    Salvation   96
Michele Leggott (New Zealand)
    Helix   97
    hyle   98
    all   99
Michael Leong (USA)
    from "Disorientations"   100
Susan Lewis (USA)
    Undeterred   105
    Rattlesnake (Lucky Strike)   107
    Keyed Out   109
Medbh McGuckian (Northern Ireland)
    Chalice Orchard   111
    Encounters with Dust   113
    A Wineskin in the Frost   115

KB Nelson (Canada)
    The Third Turtle   117
    Trap Kit   118
    Oregon Coast   119

Chris Price (New Zealand)
    Stowage   121
    Rose and fell   122
    Swan Song   124

Jon Riccio (USA)
    Visual Field   126
    Disease-iversary with Hall & Oates &   127
    The Perspectival We   128

Matthew Rohrer (USA)
    Garden of Bees   129
    Venus Waning/Apollo Waxing his Car   130
    Childhood Stories   132

Jerome Rothenberg (USA)
    Coda to a Book of Dreams   133
    "To Dream Infinity"   136
    From "In the Shadow of a Mad King"   139

Jake Sheff (USA)
    Creosote Covenant   141
    Emerson's Submarine   142
    Why Tamper with the Spectral Spoil?   143

Julia Stakhivska (Ukraine)
    Coastline   144
    Tender Is the Night   145
    Orpheus   146

Thomas Townsley (USA)
    A Month of Thursdays   147
    Tangent of Ardency   148
    Accordion-Playing Clam   149

Marc Vincenz (USA)
    Wheels of Industry   150
    On a Scale of One to Fish   151
    Riptide   152

Les Wicks (Australia)
    An Edge of Our PlanCovenant   153

Milk Beach	154
Mea Culpa	155
Joshua Marie Wilkinson (USA)	
Poem for Mathias Svalina	156
Poem for Brandon Shimoda	157
Poem for Laynie Browne	158
Jeffrey Cyphers Wright (USA)	
Topol Management Company	159
Changing Station	160
Temporary Sanity	161
Paloma Yannakakis (USA)	
To Touch Blood On Stone	162
Journal of Discontent (1)	163
Journal of Discontent (2)	164
John Yau (USA)	
A Sheaf of Pleasant Voices	165
I Heard A Man Say	167
First Language Lesson	169
Andrew Zawacki (USA)	
Collider	171
Any Other Eviction, Than The Frequent	172
Credo	173
Biographical Notes	175

Acknowledgements

Somnolent Exhumation as Canticle by Will Alexander first published in *Plinth*. *Steaming Silicate Fragmentation* and *Texas Blind Salamander Feelings* by Will Alexander first appeared in *Verse*. *Looking back on it* and *Woodpigeon* by Angela Cleland first published in *Anthropocene*. *Ps & Qs, Plateresque,* and *Tabloid* by Peter Hammial originally published in *Shot Glass Journal*. *Oedipus-Mask of an American Inventor* by Andrew Joron first appeared in *Trickhouse*. *A Lithuanian Elegy* and *Dream Debris* by Robert Kelly first appeared in *Jacket*. *A Collage Has a Thousand Mouths* by Tony Kitt from *Endurable Infinity* (The University of Pittsburgh Press, 2022); used with permission. *Twenty-Four Heavenly Snippets* by Tony Kitt from *Further Through Time* (Origami Poems Project, 2022); used with permission. Noelle Kocot, three poems from *Ascent of Mothers* (Wave Books, 2023); used with permission. Michele Leggott, three poems from *As far as I can see* (Auckland University Press, 1999); used with permission. *Oregon Coast Oregon Coast* by KB Nelson first appeared in *The Wild World*. Matthew Rohrer, three poems from *Surrounded by Friends* (Wave Books, 2015); used with permission. *Coastline, Tender Is the Night,* and *Orpheus* by Julia Stakhivska, translated by Anatoly Kudryavitsky, first published in *The Frontier: 28 Contemporary Ukrainian Poets: An Anthology* by Glagoslav Publications, 2017; used with permission. *Wheels of Industry* by Marc Vincenz first published in *The Fortnightly Review*. *Milk Beach* by Les Wicks originally published by Island Press in *The Ambrosiacs* (2009); used with permission. *Poem for Mathias Svalina* and *Poem for Brandon Shimoda* by Joshua Marie Wilkinson first appeared in *Diode*. *First Language Lesson* by John Yau was first published in *Poetry*. *I Heard A Man Say* by John Yau originally appeared in *BOMB*. *Any Other Eviction than This* by Andrew Zawacki originally published by The University of Georgia Press in *By Reason of Breakings* (2002); used with permission. *Collider* by Andrew Zawacki originally published by Counterpath Press in *Videotape*, 2013; used with permission. *Credo* by Andrew Zawacki originally published by Weslian University Press in *Anabranch*, 2014; used with permission. All the included poems used with permission from the poets.

Tangential Surrealism

The word Surrealism was coined in the summer of 1917 by the poet Guillaume Apollinaire. One of the participants of this anthology Lee Ballentine described Surrealism as a "revolution in the form of method." The art historian Dickran Tashjian inadvertently suggested the term Tangential Surrealism in his 1995 book *A Boatload of Madmen: Surrealism and the American Avant-garde: 1920-1950*, where he wrote about editors who "sought cultural goals that were sometimes derived from, sometimes at odds with, sometimes tangential to, Breton's surrealism," so their magazines became platforms for their own "cultural agendas". This term seems to have taken root.

Irish poet Ciaran O'Driscoll once stated in *Cyphers* 95 that "tangential surrealists are poets whose work connects with core Surrealism somewhat further than the extent to which a straight line connects with a circle." Are we, surrealist poets of different trends, really that different? Will Alexander wrote the following in one of his essays: "For me, language, by its very operation, is alchemical, mesmeric, totalic in the way that it condenses and at the same time proves capable of leaping the boundaries of genre."

Is Tangential Surrealism a literary movement? A system? A school of writing? Or, in the words of Maurice Blanchot, a "pure practice of existence"? It obviously exists in the field of inquiry, but does it defy understanding? Genres have to be defined. As we see it, Tangential Surrealism is about writing poems through wonder, intuition, and surprising connections. If the original surrealists of the 1930s sought to unleash the unconscious mind by bringing elements of dreams to the waking world with jarring juxtapositions, tangential poetry is more about transmutation, or associative leaps, from word to word, from phrase to phrase, and from image to image. Associative logic makes poetic leaps in imagination and mood that happen, as Robert Bly noted, "when no one is watching," i.e. when the poet's thought is up in the air, between the moment the leap started and the moment the thought reaches the place it leaps to.

Bly used the term "Leaping Poetry" to refer to surrealist and magic realist influenced works. His 1975 book *Leaping Poetry: An Idea with Poems and Translations* was a collection of essays, but the "idea" referred to in the title was about "long leaping associations" in modern poetry and drew from a range of works by international poets. Carl Phillips writes about discontinuity when he referrs to this trend as "poetry that works almost entirely by means of association—no connecting narrative pieces, often no syntactical connection, poetry that is characterized by leaps not just from stanza to stanza, but from one image to the next in ways that do not immediately make sense…"

This applies to tangential surrealist poetry to a great extent. Charles Borkhuis once remarked that "Tangential Surrealism also intensifies a linguistic or textual examination of its processes. It is not unlike waking up inside a dream that is more real than reality itself—an altered reality that is both strangely familiar and irresistibly unique. One that carries critical thought with it as it leaps over the abyss on disappearing steps… hybrids are being created, which may be considered tangential to surrealism, but may be personal to individual poets and not fall into any particular collective."

Every one of Tangential Surrealists has his own bit of poetic predisposition, or ancestry. Some of of them, notably Andrew Joron, Garrett Caples, Charles Borkhuis, George Kalamaras, Andrew Zawacki, and Jeffrey Cyphers Wright, draw on the textual emphasis of language poetry bridging the gap between Surrealist and language poetry; their language-conscious Surrealism can be described as, quoting the title of an essay by Charles Borkhuis, "writing from inside the language." Some others, like Jerome Rothenberg, Robert Kelly, John Godfrey, and Diane Wakoski, as well as the late Mark Strand and Clayton Eshleman, display a strong connection to Deep Image poetry, whereas Noelle Kocot seems to be heavily influenced by the poetry of Confessionalism, exploring such a connection in her deeply-felt lyrical writing, the kind that Charles Borkhuis identifies as the "critical lyric". John Yau's interest in gnosticism and mysticism makes his tangential Surrealism unique, too. Will Alexander, Matthew Rohrer, Andrei Codrescu, Helen Ivory, Joshua Marie Wilkinson, Lee Ballentine, Michael Leong, Marc Vincenz, as well as the late Bill Knott, James Tate and Dean Young, develop(ed) their own kinds of "tangential storytelling." Despite these individual differences all these poets are true surrealists in every meaning of this word. Tangential Surrealism is inclusive and, to a certain degree, elastic.

This book also showcases a number of non-American surrealists working in this genre, like Helen Ivory and Alison Dunhill of England, Angela Cleland of Scotland, Medbh McGuckian of Northern Ireland, Les Wicks and Peter Hammial of Australia, Chris Price and Michele Leggott of New Zealand, and KB Nelson of Canada. Surrealistm may be international in scope, but in the English-speaking countries other than the USA, Australia and, to a lesser degree, Canada it doesn't have a particularly widespread influence on contemporary writing. Quoting Alicia Ostriker, "surrealism persuades us that its world is arbitrary and questionable" (qtd. in Gillian White, *Lyric Shame* 127). Unfortunately, some poetry associations, arts authorities, and publishing companies, especially in the English-speaking European countries, have extended this approach to the border of the absurd, sometimes viewing the whole Surrealism movement and, wider, any experimental writing as a questionable, or even a dangerous trend. Such mindless conformity with the mainstream status quo is as saddening as it is maddening and as ridiculous as it is futile. After all, who has the capacity to stop the development of poetry on any "God's little acre"? "It is impossible to write today as though Surrealism never existed," Jean-François Bory remarked. Well, in Francophone countries they do know it!

"After the war we witness the death of language as it was known," Henri Chopin once wrote, but the truth is that the language is always alive, even if poetry is hardly so. Lettrism and other attempts to dismantle words, which are the core of a language, didn't really take root, even though they heavily influenced visual poetry and contributed to its development. Every new generation of poets has to learn afresh how to use the language in innovative, unexpected ways, and they always succeed in doing that. Guided by their surrealistic imagination, they tend to go deeper and wider, to explore the horizons of ambience.

We didn't include any translated work in this book – with one exception: we believed that poems by the Ukrainian writer and artist Julia Stakhivska deserve to be in it. Julia is not the only poet belonging to the younger generation of surrealists: we also introduce such accomplished authors as Clayre Benzadón, Lily Brown, Charles Kell, Jon Riccio, Jake Sheff, and Pamela Yannakakis.

Surrealism has seen many revivals since André Breton's first manifesto of 1924. Its new revival is more or less recent: the

International Society for the Study of Surrealism was established in 2018; it attempts, quoting their mission statement, to "integrate the field of Surrealism studies worldwide by organizing events and managing channels of information that facilitate cross-disciplinary and inter-regional communication and exchange." In 2022, *Contemporary Surrealist and Magic Realist Poetry* anthology edited by Jonas Zdanys was published by Lamar University Press in Texas, USA. It was an imporant achievement in researching the possible surrealist practices across the globe. In the future, further steps can – and should – be taken in anthologising different trends of contemporary Surrealist writing. This particular anthology is an attempt to gather together the poets whose Tangential Surrealism, we believe, deserves an exporatory look.

Tony Kitt
Dublin, Ireland, August 2023

WILL ALEXANDER (USA)

Steaming Silicate Fragmentation

Perhaps
more crystalline
than interior translucence
than marbled coracle phantoms
sailing across a fulminated bay of seals
paradoxically alive
as troubling lenticular power

this being the sight strained
to such a degree
that the voice loses foci
with its sorcerous animal whirlings
with its colubrine nightmares
with its sound from a muted ravens' wick

the sight with its feverish structural power springing from a phlogotic oxygen
from the minerals of inverse Martian blazes

this being the biaxial as crystal
something other than Saturnian
being orectic fire as the substance of Mars

Texas Blind Salamander Feelings

Its sonar glowing
its eyes
inverted aphid's scrolls
having taken on the tenor of nautical-turpentine sparks
creeping reptilian polyps
being sulphur as in-lunation
not unlike flameless snow fields re-inverting
being the dialectical polarity
of magma
being molten underground intarsias
their movement
not unlike the wind from a primitive whispering axe

one thinks of the electro-chimerical firing of axons
of open optical annihilation pulsing through phantoms of
emptiness

again one thinks of deserted centaur colonies
of hidden retinal satin
of juniper vines distorted as ionized cometary hair

the latter being an abstract fovea
invisible cortical cells
akin to their liquifous genes
to the rote that moves through their strange genetic calliope

this being sight
not unlike prophecy
or shapeless bells in the mirror of the skin catching fire as
somnific vibration

as Antarctic anaemia
like the Irminger current
or the deep barbarian steam within rubies

& the opera
inside its flesh shapes
a strange refractive iodine gone missing

Somnolent Exhumation as Canticle

This lonely extended choir of singing
as curious insouciant wavering gone blind
being a bloody complicitous sun gone blind running the gamut of its own
extended fire not unlike explosive dolomite invasion
being a spine of rocks burning upwards into inflammatory metrics
being involuntary wind
being a store house of spiders
perhaps a monarch of bones rising as inspired green tin inside ice
    infected
molecules of fire
perhaps exacting zodiac waters obtusely engendered in league
with violent abstracted velvet oscillations branded as a proviso of
    corpses
cooked with radiation
prowling in refrangible horse sleep ethers

JOHN THOMAS ALLEN (USA)

Dust

Smoking patio
breathing pine bush
leaves of green razor.

The March leaf hanging like a crippled
butterfly—

A starless morning,
the cuffed breeze,
a sky's crisp condescension,
the blueness of your monster:

To speak in taxidermy,
empty sound bytes,
Christabel feathers

ringing in fall...

your mouth reeling celluloid
stuffed with black feathers. I
will not see you long again, it
should grow dark tonight.

You will talk your way back into it.

Roswell Construction

In the desert
we wear tinfoil caps

As it grows warmer
The beads spill down our faces
bits of a rock salt rosary

Breaks are taken
when it rains

for sand dune novenas
We drink and pray to mosaics
made eyeless by white sand

sandblasted by lattice waves
Light congregates
on each man's head

from one altitude to the next
above and below
endlessly

The Lighthouse above the Graveyard

I am the keeper, the manager
of dim-wick ammonia. Blue goblets

rage at noontide, varicose flowers
bloom; an old woman's leg

walking to kneel. I wind solvents
for yard lines running in butterfly wings,

tracing their crippled beats,
keeping score. Pure iodine

and enunciate palmistry
(along with a little love)

is what keeps my sedate island
in good order. Bumps in the sand

knock and knock; I get around
most nights. It can be beautiful

watching the tide
kiss our namesakes away
and bells chime,
a cowled figure in a half trance
listens to the forest's groan,
the creaking bark,
a dusty cough,
a prisoner moaning in his cell.

LEE BALLENTINE (USA)

Solecipsism

my cellphone is my dog's bark when puzzled

I talk a little louder than conceivably necessary
before the accident

I don't exist and you I hypothecate

my dog's bark when puzzled

recorded this conceivably necessary way of showing off
my tattoos

no substitution is my scheme, schema
of the invisible self

ringing, buzzing, can you hear me?

The Dead Body and the Living Body

in a gesture particular to him, zorro took
the lovely dead body and the lovely living body
and blindfolded himself to see if he could
enumerate their differences blindfolded

the living, upon being touched lightly
with the handle of the saber
uttered a "quack" and the dead, unprompted
uttered the same "quack"

and taking off his blindfold, zorro
looked at his oscilloscope
and saw that indeed the two "quacks"
were virtually identical

and the dead sat up and said
"you know pal, if you cut a couple of holes
in that black blindfold
you could see everything without taking it off . . ."

and zorro walked out of the lab
leaving the bodies behind
and leaving behind the country of the vaqueros
and leaving the country of the ranchos

and leaving behind the sun and the moon
and the seashells made of fear
and the stones of blood
and the limp of the bull in the small corrida

and leaving the campesinos
and leaving the revolution
and the books about it
and the daguerrotypes of the generals

and leaving behind the nearby village
and its old fruiterer
and the young meat cutter
with his red-stained shirt

and the power outages on the coast
and the hotel lobbies
lit only by starlight
and the bodies locked in embrace

and he rode north to where his US cousins
tiny creatures
gathered around an oval table
every afternoon for supper

and listened to the old RCA radio
that was bigger then they were
and he stood in line at the motor vehicles
and took a number

still wearing his blindfold
with the two holes cut out

and that is how all the brouhaha began

The Fou-Gou

will you make this posture?
the head folded down
the fist genuflects
the legs hold their tongue

the body is full of infinitesimals
whirlpools, spores, rain
the body is rain falling or if a groan, whose?
I stand at the gate of horn, entry the skew of it
the middle house I ascend, descend
my entry solitaire, rotation of dissenting sky
cover my head with dust of candlesight

the fou-gou is a house underground
house occipital
house of houses knowing
house of missing voices
house retrograde
I walk up, walk down axis of melancholy

dried sweat and river longing
the bed made, unmade
and graveclothes twisted
memorize that other year, other river
one mournful and tepid
one gone black in glint
of pallid distempers, distastes
quotient of light and satellite

a crenellated vision of ants
their slow rush together
walk up, walk down, melancthony
I would know if not much kept me
wait quickly
not seeing prayers smoke and dissipate
and rob dead stones of their paralyses
the sound of accidental sight
that kind of theater

CLAYRE BENZADÓN (USA)

Ephemera

In one day, a mare
rams into a hare, seizes
it, pares its skin with her teeth.

She bows into dimness,
peers into hampered eventide
to find ephemeron: mayfly, double
adult and life-
cycle flyfished

with bucktail, handled
by a figures' back cast,
tip of the rod upwards,
leaving surface dark

on a young blue giant,
bluefish turned into rare star.

Harm burns there, above,
in the blueshifted sky,

where polar rabbits'
tracks are blueprinted,
tied with a blood knot.

There, the atmosphere
shifts through multiple
stages of development,

instars, nymphal
form fossilized,
like the insect

hatched into
plasmatic matter,
until it passes,
charging through,

attaining imago.

Honeydew

Honeydew silence.

Outside the weeds
taste honey, lie

wedding dew, new
line settled into
a different abandon.

First feel of breath
current. Certain things

rent out surrender, like
a den without its rooster,

storeless rest. I've seen
summer become senile
before, now harvest saves

nectar vest over grass
labor: a comb, suckle,

care of another suckling
wild boar, drinking deter-
minately tearing neat and

near until milk
turns into honey-
dew.

Wheatfield Treehouse

Wheatfield for miles.
White heat feeds the weeds durably.
The feet that land on the stalks
lead onto the marsh, eat the malt

and the leftovers, held
in between toes, wielding
spikelets like claws.

There is only you
in the grain maze.
Stalk heads split
sideways, hold

themselves like electric
slits. After silence
comes terror.

A life fit for lightning people.
Buckets fill with bearded
cartwheels.

The only lane of desert
in pollen is umber
teddy bear treehouse,

an antique
lace rarity,

bolt of soft
red winter.

CHARLES BORKHUIS (USA)

Face the Music and Dance

I wonder if I might borrow your face for a while
I mean the one you're not using at the moment
you know the witty life-of-the party type
or maybe the sensitive good listener
who goes the extra mile because he cares
or the strong silent frankie knuckles type
who puts the lean on poets that don't pay up

or maybe I won't go out today
maybe I won't face the dissonant atonal
music of the street and its loyal discontents
of which I am one

besides to step out the door requires
a frontal lobotomy of sorts
your multiples must collapse into a false unity
that drives the apparatus
which forces us to make sense
of a world that withdraws every time
we treat it like a tool

face it talking to yourself in public
may result in hostile stares
and forced removal from the premises
but wouldn't it be interesting to be in a room

with others whose inner voices talked to each other
and everyone dropped the sham
that you are only you
and that this projected world is all there is

Further Instructions

let's say a body falls
head first into wave upon wave of roiling voices
a harsh hello here a sweet goodbye there
it all gets tangled up in the gurgle and foam
of so many swarming targets
searching for the right arrow

each to his own half-held beliefs
reincarnation placed upon a shelf
next to a can of pork and beans
a logbook of meaningful coincidences
leans against a jar of rusty keys
which door to what metaphor

no need to panic
most ideas only go so far
then someone blows a whistle
and you pick yourself up off the ground
maybe we're not made to get
to the heart of the matter
maybe nothing sticks around that long

might as well catch the next wave
of fluttering digressions or half-baked ideas
listen closely for a secret code in their banter
nudging us closer to the truth but never quite
close enough to hear matter mumbling as it turns
into light yet the transformation often occurs
while we're thinking of something else

it's no secret that words
are watching us from a distance
waiting to switch narratives or bite
maybe it's unavoidable that we are thrown
into situations that are beyond us
that we must stand for something
we don't fully understand
and act upon it with our lives

Witness

witness the limits once again
old blade of forms the lines on a face

cut from a playing card
that may one day talk back to you

song of the inkblot growing inside the man
the beast he so effortlessly becomes

how like an angel perched on a precipice
a paradox hanging coyly from a branch

just to let him know he'll never know enough
to keep the demons out

the train wheels from screeching
sentences from marching ceaselessly forward

locking his jaw in a cage
where words once rolled freely off his lips

what was revealed will wither in time
only to reappear as a phantom of memory

with no witness to confirm these comings
and goings they scurry across the eye

one of life's most ordinary creatures
calls you by name witness to his failings

his secret animal stirrings
how as a boy he suffered under a stiff collar

and wrote on a blackboard his offense
over and over till the words enlarged

into meaningless bars behind which he paced
dreaming his escape

LILY BROWN (USA)

Socket

Out of a ripped situation, we learned
to boat. Tacked once the harbor
in a wood-ribbed float
then curved to port.

I remember twirling through air,
a baton in pain, then an arm
backed into its socket
by a doctor.

Knocked into structure,
I open my bones. I could
go about it
differently, but what good

is rattling in a basket?
And is it waiting
if you don't know
after is what you'd want?

Leaf at the End

I climbed a giant leaf at the end
of my imagination. Across
the spotted water, the hill
fastened its yellow bushels.

The imagination asked for all the cities,
for the canopy to get its machines out
and tile the leaves. My friend Lily
assumes what I want and it's so unfair.

The imagination shoves in and pushes
blithely out, a belt of pelicans, a plank
of hard clouds, bunches of doorknobs
halo the street-blighted hills.

I find a pile of antlers in the woods, assembled
for burning. I crawl beneath them and stay
there when the burners come with their fire.
Up in the canopy I dangle, touching nothing.

Its Character

This could be a photo of wood, black ink
scored across it. The cracks are real.
No, wood's plied into a shape.

Remove the paper.
Green spine meets black
face in a lifted ridge.

We've restored the original,
one-poem-per-page model. The original?
I face the wall. My back to the dead-bug

curtains and their tale of white.
I'm elsewhere. Sounds let up at the top
and fade. I have a radiator full of water.

It could be bad for my health, everything
with plugs, unidentified in the hedge.
Authentic stamps on the floor. I turn across

the bed. I need shelves, I need storage. I need
to stop who you are. In the fantasy
head, you always write. It happened that 1pm

passed and she signed her letters with one word,
then five words, then three words, then six.
Unroll your quarters-in-paper, poem

in a bad time. I'm in the wilds without
my feet. In the slick cedar swamp,
all is a primitive green. The lightless thicket

where even the air's hung up
and colored, the tree line sticks the clouds.

GARRETT CAPLES (USA)

Sundial Tone

after Alfred Starr Hamilton

light plays on the planet
long enough to tell time

the bird tells time by the sundial
the sundial by the bird

time will tell the bird a tale
the sundial's never heard

a tale as long as the riverbank
from here to the hydroelectric plant

man-o-man, the bird will think
as it sails above the river

the plant is not a plant
the bank is not a bank

the bird alights on a branch
of the river, the bank, a tree

the bird leaves the tree leaves
behind on the stage

of the play it pages through

André Breton's Apartment

the madder runs
like blood

lifeblood of
the livebud

that kindles next to earth

the hair on the church is water
the lovebirds curve their crutches down

so long
to the sacred
palaces

so long to the fingerbone that lingers on

if i'm alive
it's no thanks to you

if i'm comatose
let's make the most of it

tomato ghost

rude twilight

ruby tear

discipline disappears

between the shapeless necklace
and the cloudy robe of shrapnel

in the absence
of incense

no balm can grease
the throbbing temples

of the rotting world

Ordinary History America

the trapdoor is closed; am finite again, but a moment ago—
                              levitation!
purple lights the bluewater bridge turned on the oil-
black river st clair became fuel for the nightfishers there
it was the dream of a memory or the memory of a dream
that dumped me below a window, watching a woman change
into a man. she entered his dairy log: at first all the world was
                              america
and didn't that suck, he thunk, and strunk his cunk against
an overwrought iron fence. they stood waiting like that photograph
of the bootblack jack and the aristocrat
looking away from her window
at a fact well worth recording—Alexander Graham Bell wanted
                              to call
his daughter Photophone. between the forest and the gander
i hand her over to Metacomet. yes i certainly did.
and King Philip sayeth unto me: nature denatured thee
friction alone makes her come therefore i need some more
before you make me wear'um pants. O failed invention!
where'd you get that voice? refusing to come
to a particular point, castration finally made sense.

ANGELA CLELAND (Scotland)

Cross

Needling of jabs, riddle of ducks and feints,
you wait for a clear target.

It comes, as brief as a spark plug's discharge,
as a flash of knicker. You unload

from the pivoting toes of the back leg,
extend through knee, hip, ribs, shoulder, elbow –

you are industrial, a piston, oiled
metal pain. Misjudge

and your attack could be countered,
your nose smacked ice pack absent numb,

worse, your blow could absorb like melt water
into the padding of your opponent's gloves.

Looking back on it

They were like horse clippings,
like burning holes in the world.
Snapped pretzels raining from the sky.
I knew what it meant, of course:
they were coming as priests do
to collect our easy meat, to coddle us,
to shave our incredulity, wearing
pretext like a spangled mitre – oh!
they wanted to be frosted tyrants.
Or, it wasn't that at all,
it was that the lake was all treacle,
was perfectly calm. Not the lake,
the horse. It was nothing to do
with the cold hard nuggets
of freeze-dried wood that sat in our hearts.
Our hearts that were falling –
wait! It was not our hearts,
it was our livers and they were
not falling, but failing so
we sat without bile in the face of it all.
Of course, you could have sharpened swords
on his self-confidence. Of course
those regrets were nothing like any of this.
They were countless empty spindles
turning end-on in the night sky.

Woodpigeon

I am tasked with finding the source of the music
and do not refuse, though it's true I doubt
the Ministry of Hope's intentions.

The concern is that it may be birdsong,
but I don't buy that. I've heard a bird
recorded - it was high and clear.

Following the sung trail, I'm a bead
sailing down a length of thread,
round with purpose, toes barely

skiffing tarmac, light as I pass
above the smudged, upturned faces
of the children of the reclamation.

They pause their vital work to watch me
from beneath the pavement grates.
It feels good to work.

The sky is a rusty tin can lid, painted
fairly convincingly, I think,
to look like a long-lost summers' day.

Shadows lengthen as I follow
out and on and on out to the suburbs,
the deconstructed suburbs,

past concrete structures brutalised
by muscular plant life,
an entropic paradise.

The repeated phrase of music brings me
here, to what was once a square
akin to those that survive in the nub.

The walls are scaled with ivy, the pillars
become trees circumscribing a glade.
Trolleys gather here for safe grazing.

Semblance. There is no bird. Just the flap
of wet canvas in the breeze and a breathy voice
haunting the ruins of the roofless Co-op,

all the emotion fallen out of it,
enunciation dissolved by its mad repetition:
I don't want to go. I don't want to go.

ANDREI CODRESCU (USA)

The Best Side of Me

Tomatoes squashes and cauliflowers intrigue me immensely
with their lewd proposals
and their making the stability of my appetite burst
with the lust of their red yellow and white chewiness.
You're chewy, I'm loony.
I dream of soft furry things with inward claws
lodged in my brain
who open when it rains.
Then whole cities built around a glob of waving squash.
We float backwards into early tickles of consciousness.
Faces pull though complicated threads of greasy smiles.
My friend peter chewing on his model airplane,
the stretched frown of my tomato nanny.
If I ever let go of this dream
my work is all over. My body releases
the captives of ten thousand labors

Bicycle

Touch that spoke while it spins
at the world exhibition in Paris as all
the characters of sentimental novels
who have fled their master's manuscripts
with Morcol the detective of shadows
in hot pursuit being recorded by M. Queneau
are mounting the bicycle seat one by one
and deciding their destinies in a fulgurant second.
The appeal and the description by later
exegetic apologists for the postmodern
takes longer than we thought and besides
nobody dares touch the spoke as the wheel
spins not even the talented ones whose hands
have been slapped by something we'll call
culture or hypnosis or techno-somnolence.
Meanwhile time flies and nobody's having fun.

Truth & Ruffles

I now have a compulsion to enter man terrain
with the pitchfork ready.
The gravity in leaves pulls at the round thumping
in my palms, the random
beat of living figs
behind newspapers.
It is this compulsion I'm giving you
for the best film
of our time.
I am truly my inherited proposition.
Out here, out there

ALISON DUNHILL (England)

Ice Moon

I pull back from falling into the rocked crevice of love
by girding my loins with a cloth
of words soaked in wax and bitumen.

I skate-dance on ice, a solitary star,
backgrounded by Canary Wharf's skyline.
I dazzle, my feet spark, they're hung with bells.

You watch from every corner in turn, unimpressed,
eating ice cream.
While the Thames tide turns, questions flash crossette fireworks
      on the horizon.

Will the famous bridge rise?
Is the moon full? Are you ready? Do you want another one?

Cloud Construction

Lines of crystals strewn over Wondermesh. Stars in the night sky. Constellations of city lights on 'islands' on a night flight. Wondermesh clouds, plaster and textile clouds, hanging and light-filled, moving in space, their transparency stopped by small bits of consumer waste. Blue clouds, black cloud, in netting or mesh, threads stretched, draped and coiled with flowers and leaves on silk devorée remnants. Mini-clouds in textile-pierced plaster: a flock of flying wall duck-clouds. Nebulous edges of unmoulded plaster, studded with copper pipe, glass beads. Volcanic craters in symmetry. Miniature Doric columns with coloured ribbon-tied, tiny scrolls; Temple of Segesta. My columns encasing secrets in their scrolls, a nod to ancient writing templates. Each scroll a small unit in a growing multiple.

White pillars, gold pillars, wild, flying, multi-textile, green
    pillars.
Clouds made by pouring plaster onto sand piles.
    Gouging,
paint-streaking, embedding the plaster form with glass,
    metal and
textile offcuts. Working fast before the plaster dries.
    City street
bits, squashed and bent by a thousand lorries in Rio, a
    rusty pile of the disused
once useful. Dull aluminium, verdigrised copper, bright
    new copper,
duller brass, matt zinc, cheap tin glints like silver – silver-
    coated plastic.

Fountain

She was there, but wraith-like, iris soft-eyed;
her dream outside these walls, her hopes a sticky layer.
Furniture around her,

    green fountains of leaves outside.

Not moving amongst the furniture.
Crescent smiles, spun-gold eyes of friends,
the colours of life condensed for keeping.

    The tip of a larch tree dangles its silhouette over a cloud.

Spring's new fullness brought sadness again.
Dry brown earth turned pink with
speckled horse chestnut dropped flower.

    Sweet evening sun palely lights a twist of trunk

and now the green hands of leaves sway and flicker
as she sits in the room's half light
watching rhododendron's candyfloss.

JOHN GODFREY (USA)

Pink Tab

Baloney of superstar grade
    On board with night movies
        Man-made time so nosey

Dark enough to drive in
    Won't bore you, my memories
        Things don't just happen

Notes play, I'll be there
    You know solar? Like that
        Now hear play of shadows

If I hear her I can see
    Now pick up pink tab
        My pleasures blush and blush

Have to pay to cross streets
    Winter clothes not always
        That face, for instance, profound

Light Years Ago

Infants hold out their pants
    and sing
Sun spanks a spaceship
    light years ago
For too long I have asked
    this city to be
    great with child
and off the pace

Curtain reaches into
    me like droplets
Forward go the gears
    and the paint job ripples
To the left we pass places
    yet to be lived in
They are full of my memories
    which one day they share

All the shocks absorbed
    under jungle
Running feet on handrail
    Inverted pyramid
    of leotards
I must sleep like a watchman
    to revere the antic
There's a provocatrice
    somewhere in
    my coat
When she rises in her sleep
    to walk

stairs, to protect her
      sleep more alertly

Find some other dregs
      is one thing to say
on the night side
      of morning
A voice with an air
      finds its way in
Puts a hold on messages
      for now
         from regret

Can You Tell

Happens this time
in answer to indecency
Lit by the yellow
shop windows cast
Unkind to you, that light
You say, Sit, Ubu, sit, or
Hey, I like your weave

This avenue for instance
Gateway to escapade
You can see from the
beginning to its end
All-embracing greed
Distracting appliqués
of altruism
Small pomme de terre
Can you tell whose
hand on the basinet
and that does what for you

Warmth all in the light
Sight all in
garage park hallway
Morning's dusk on pause
You stand body in profile
What you don't fill
in the doorway stays empty
More than overcome
I know you're there
and unseal my lips

PHILIP HAMMIAL (Australia)

Ps & Qs

Between wet Elvis & dry Elvis
I stand corrected
by Madam. Mind
my Ps & Qs: Peccadillos &
Quadraphonics. On cue: Gather
it in, the harvest, its faucet
in mother's closet jammed open. That my sailor
might survive in this sea she's prepared to open
a shark's belly with her teeth. Welcome
aboard, welcome to the rendering, the insouciance
of which will curtail any evacuation, even of
that effigy which his Holiness would squeeze out
for the Mass, for those widows who would project
an image of modernity & obviously fail, their kitchens
given over to scullions who make the best of what can
only be described as a chronic penile disfunction. Pick
your own peck of peppers, boys; I've got
better things to do. Like? Like
get it right, how I stand, cuffed, rump out
between a wet & a dry Elvis.

Plateresque

Be bedizened if you may, if that a fate
you unbidden to
choose. As for me,
I'd like to bray & sooth

some say & bowdlerize some harvest
I could not otherwise script
or own up to, some lucky lamentation
that might so unterre me that from

some quantum of aloof labour
I could expect a satisfying scratch not
previously announced, a lifting
lilting touch upon my speech-
profaning self (humble now)
who only yesterday would feign
a mere taste lapse to explain my lack
of bedazzlement in verse.

Tabloid

My mother? I'm wearing her as tight as I can, as
I always have in that house of religious purpose. Some
purpose, Death for a laugh when in fact
it's an exercise in cross-dressing taken to a conga line
length, a Golden Mile of would-be starlets scratching & tearing
until they're through to the other side, to: Zenshin
A-rippu kosu (a full-body A-lip course), Yoko shouting
Yam sentence! Yam sentence! while I swallow my pride
& get on with it. Note: when Yoko roars yours
truly a tumble in the hay takes with Betty, full-blooded
American girl, just to get back. Spiteful bastard, O just
to get back I do, I do. What Yoko deserves, her cupboard
far from bare, her rendezvous with the wall-eyed assassin
on the Street of the Unhorsed Imam, her commercial plight
with legs to match, her horde of urine in bedside bottles, her moth-
eaten collection of beaver tails. I'm thinking of wearing her too.

ROBERTO HARRISON (USA)

nocturnal heritage

then when they offered something
of command, the night
received them to confirm
a change of season. they were not
standing on the earth, or
they remembered that the fields of rice
would not harvest them, people
of the ashes. their directions
would not receive the ancient winds
or the doorway to the past
brought them firmly to the soil. they were often
not known
by number, and they were once
attached to the after years
of service. they did not
announce themselves
as their words
would not serve the ashes. and they once
had their memories
grown for the fields
of their pockets. no one
could speak
after they moved
on the soil
through the oceans

eat white

idiot moon
I vacillate

with fevers
and fear

and no one hears
my engine

silent
animal.

all art
is gone

for the penetrative
climate

more rocks
for the feet

of the fern.
we migrate

to touch
the apostles

of nature
with their removed

faces
and a worn door

done
by numbers

dearest animal

dearest faun, the approach to the weather
that others portray as we see the adorned, the material

captioning that the forest undoes for witness, of what is seen
and what is absorbed by the flesh of the wind, none of those

disasters or the war, and none of the Sea will write it to the unformed
as someone of the other field attends to your received oblivion

an eclipse of your offering, of your desire to remain outside all consciousness
in the weather that attends to your gift of wandering, all the fields

and the groups are yours in this focus of the soil, of the insects, of our
detriment that the offers of reconciliation and their more new organs

of the possible. those who cradle in their appeasement of the storms
and raid the antlers that hold your secondary wakefulness, like all others

in their fuse for the climate of Return. dear animal, you cause me to float
those openings where we emerge as a climbing symbol

as those who attend to your eyes and your feet, for a cut inside
by the knives of semblances and by the origins of our increasing abscess

to remain like the mountain of an encroaching pocket
and like the hold of its arms of the few to the path of the worn

NICHOLAS ALEXANDER HAYES (USA)

Ghost Lineage

A pluripotent shepherd moon
clears a path through ephemera
leaving traces but not bones.

Call infinite reds shift home.

Despite equilibrium of orbit,
lines of causality never
intersect in the pit.

Keep planetoids with meteors.

Look for iron flare

to scrape
membranes free of
fur and folly.

Chewing tanners collapse
wave function
as they keep hide supple.

Root to Nourish Love

Eyes become milky sea.

We tread particle waves,
waiting for a life raft.

Slow days sprout
as the pineal gland
stretches toward

an abandoned city
on a hill,

echoing with tuatara.

Panspermia

Strike your cane against
the void to see
manna
flow

sweet like
divinity cooling on the
breezeway on a
clear winter day

in yellow fields
encroached by locust thickets.

Cup your hand below
my beard to
see if you can
hold a swarm,

a pestilence
of unspoken words

of lost affectations.

STEFANIA HEIM (USA)

A Large Mirror Unloaded From a Truck in the Sun

Participation relegated to sleeping near
the open window. My great failure

has always been not imagining the future
but in managing myself. Your thumbprint, please,

before we launch the new rhetoric. I know
when I grovel I am plain. I've actually had a dream

about this building, and it feels soon enough to me now.
For all the reasons we are short of breath, approximate.

Passion clusters as though circumstance. A terrible
child, I grow apart. According to the original

rules, burn everything. Who could have anticipated
what we are becoming—in constraint, in circumspection.

I'll think of some experiment to move us,
focusing on the lenses learned.

From "HOUR BOOK": 3:49PM

The same frog strum is punctuating
time. I remember when because the measure

of life is now child-stick – significantly
shorter ruler, impossibly laden. Before

but just barely. I couldn't see
so far, like to the mountains beyond the ridge of shifting

tree-line. One field's bee is improbably attracted
to a bright blue chair, though there are flowers.

A stranger with a knife and bowl gathers herbs. Driving,
I am equally discomfited by a car close behind as by

the absence of cars. Without markers
I do not trust that the road is fixed. Sitting now, just trying

not to suffocate on big country time. Counterproject,
counter-instinct, trying not

to mark it. It would be so quiet but for the frog.
Nature makes such difficult lines.

Sometimes a syncopated strum, a
double.

From "HOUR BOOK": 6:35PM

Slide projector rain in the space
of sought solitude. Wishing
for leaf shadows that are ever-more

distinct. I came at the appointed
time, but that time was an error.

How do you understand
objects enough to proffer them? An errant
hand caught on film. A fantastical bridge.

How do you decide how to decide?
And what is the appropriate

posture of attention?

BOB HEMAN (USA)

The Story Of

the story of
was a man
replaced with numbers

a line drawn
where no line
had been before

a map folded
so that it
all made sense

The Distance

the distance between
or the man running
his own voice chasing him
until he is able

the surface of
only where the sea
seems to begin or end

his name given to him then

One Becomes

one becomes only
what is necessary

the ocean sometimes
or a frog
or door

the man painted
so that he resembles

the woman a shadow
if she is even seen

the machine
never turned on

HELEN IVORY (England)

The Square of the Clockmaker

When the last train left,
the tunnel rolled the train track
back into its mouth and slept.

Clocks unhitched themselves
from the made-up world of timetables
and opened wide their arms.

And in the square of the clockmaker
a century of clocks
turned their faces to the sun.

Sister

The moon is weary of the City's halogens
and neon flamingos;
its spangling vauntings of plastic glamour.

If the moon could anthropomorphicise itself
she would be a sister in a hospital drama
with judgemental eyebrows and sanitized hands.

She would stand at the edge of the ward
one eye on the casino
the other on the pelican crossing.

She would summon the sea
to this landlocked place
and tuck it in snug with hospital corners.

The Art Gallery

clears its throat and holds forth
to the symposium's audience
of one hundred and twenty stacking chairs,
a water cooler with seven plastic cups, and a broom.

Is it a given then, that these Old Masters
are shorn of their aesthetic and their monetary value
when there are no human eyes to feast here?
it asserts, getting into its stride.

The water-cooler gurgles crankily in response,
the broom agitates the dust
while the faces on the walls look
as they have looked for tongue-tied centuries.

ANDREW JORON (USA)

Oedipus-Mask of an American Inventor

Trapped among the mirrored leaves
Of his life story
    the time-traveller returns
To drown his infant father

– he enters the farmhouse
Weeps
    before a family tableau
That circle of elders
Like unhewn blocks

Roof is gone, blown away
In the storm that made the world

Night-sky
Pales to the north
    beyond the badlands
As if a Metropolis were rising there

He wanders through deserted
    rooms, trailing
An army of alternative selves

In his decelerated state
    hearth-flames are icicles
That splinter to the touch

He holds
    one light-shard aloft
Inspects the furniture of bone
& stretched skin

The white larva

Lies curled in its crib
    flicking its tail

The newborn scalp
    feels papery-thin
Construct of Bible & dinosaur
Egg

    swept by time-waves
The text devolves
To a tangle of hieroglyphs

A fossil
Sinking through stone

Assumption, The

Climb, the
Premise, the –
What drama
    of the size of signs, of sighs
Seized at zero.
A dry soul is best
    because combustible –
But to stand
    beyond witness, burying the sun
    or else writing fire
    along a circumference of unclosing
– this is my faith & my reason.
I enter history
As a secret agent or stone effigy
    dedicated to communism
    but eaten away by music.
My chorus
    vacuum-crowded, I
    beg to begin –
If now
    is a precipice, then
A human voice predates the universe.
Everything sends, never to receive
This message
Premonitory to a shriek – of
Shredded
    immensité the vocable, irrevocable
    Proof.

Boreal

Across the stiffening pond, your steps
    send broken branching signals
Faultless as some harp-tuning

    dedicated to silence: each note
Carries an interior candle of dissonance
    the dark calendar
Marked by a sequence of frozen suns

There is a season deeper than winter
Passing in these
    tree-diagrams, & mechanisms
Of common speech

Sleeping under the solstice, you may suffer
Recurrent dreams
    as the wreckage returns its image

Unburied
The harp
    a pelvic bone, turns in your hands

But failing (you—the player
Of a misshapen instrument)
    to complete the world's anatomy

(That story was told in deafening peals)
    or even to mimic this

Weather's argument-in-whispers, its subtle
    ashen-green
Striations...

"Let waters once chaotic
    assume the form of a rigid plane"

    understanding things
    are furious in their motionlessness

If the laws that govern *awakening*
Come to resemble a city of blue spires

    you will not awaken soon

GEORGE KALAMARAS (USA)

The Fourth Way In

Now we come to copper in the throat.
We come to condolences. We come to regret.

We were kept busy by mounds of buckled soil.
We knew the trek would be difficult, but we undertook it anyway for
twenty camel loads of tea.

Rapidly, I wanted to utter my own name with complete confidence.
The yogi told me days before to instead say, Brilliant me my mouth.

I'll confess it this way: when I came into this world, I was baptized in
the stain of a mulberry tree.
In other words, when we entered the kitchen, it was the kitchen that
was hungry.

You don't believe there were four alternatives, one of which was to
enter India through our own way of breathing?
In the dream, someone placed a candle into my left ear and lit it with
fossilized rainwater.

About nine miles from the oasis, I swallowed a small black stone.
No cure, no craving, no coupling to this life I had somehow grown to
call my own.

The Sorrow of Listening

This breath that keeps my breath is a living swell.
Music, maps, and motivations have guided me back life upon life.

The month before my birthday each year is an obstinate weed.
I must not have wanted to return this time to this unsure ground.

I think of a beautiful evening of almost-solid air.
The sorrow of listening to a box of cigars in their wrappers exacts a stiff reply.

What might we say, and how might we sway it through our mouths?
I hear distant drumming as if email does not exist.

The photograph of the beehive actually smelled of honey.
Go to your life, I heard. *Comb the labyrinth. Scratch its beard of intoxicating sea lice. See what wanton waters you can most willfully waste.*

This Roundness of Now

Then it was musk in the noise of my mouth.
I had swollen so many wounds unto myself.

I might speak the sudden wind chime of a bee.
I might resolve myself in circles of could and maybe and won't.

When the body is bitten into birth by the fire ants of Namibia.
When griffon vultures descend upon what needs to be ever more
    cleanly broken.

If you ask me my name in one of the three lost languages of salt, I
    might say, *Here, this roundness of now.*
If you deceptive and quarrel and shift.

Please, take the most tender parts of my words into you and feel the
    heron content of your blood expand with the ebullient grief of
    my most human.
Look me in the eye, with *all* of your mouths. Cry out into the leaves.
    Bring the wingèd bleed of the sycamores from you into me.

CHARLES KELL (USA)

Asp

Feel my shape—fossil
back from black ash

to a picture on the mantel.
Out of that zinc sheet

into a hot bubble. Out of steel
steps dripping white

paint, green skin tossed
off along the rail. Out of names,

nickel, ampersand. The marriage
of tongue to salt back to chilled

aluminum. You were catching
my breath for hours on end.

Dead Letter Office

Work papers bound in blue string;
ink covers the table, runs over

a slanted floor; keyholes rattle in a cold New
Bedford wind. Here, in my mouth again.

Sweating barrel of an empty bottle.
Phlegm from a November catarrh.

This is the *Etching of Plague Years.*
Barbed wire, tourmaline, lye soap.

The sister text that began with
The Book of Salt, Sand & Rope.

A fly spins on a sheet of white melamine.
A fly is frozen in a glim of ice.

Ambergris

Here, underwater, bubbles are bells.
Whales are cathedrals
who spin in coruscating kelp
while we mimic the ribs of divers,
this one paper lantern
barrel
behind foil-wrapped oleander.
ing toward
the bottom of the sea.

I chew tinfoil.
Here, in Bruges, bells
are soaked in salty brine.
I kill time.
Tiresias counts important green pebbles.
See my scabs shine

ROBERT KELLY (USA)

A Lithuanian Elegy

for Jonas Mekas

Mist mist my beauty lost
I hear an old man talking

We must be woods
Wise women tied ribbons to branches

The wind knows how to read
So much water in this little river

Don't lose the old religion Moon
We are strong because we need

Sometimes a father's older than his son
Did you hear the sermon on the broken guitar

I have taught my daughter the names of trees
Touch no one till the sun goes down

You saw a man bleeding on the river bank
We wash and wash and never come clean

We know each other by the way we walk
Red ribbons like strips of meat in the rain.

Dream Debris

And when there's nothing left there's you
you cast a shadow that makes me.
The dreadful two of us again, mother
and son, father and daughter, broken
down the middle like an old barn,
christ, owls and woodchucks live therein
and all the bad birds celebrate their spring

but it's australia down in here, a metal
language and faces with big pores
staring straight into the sun, where money lives
shaped like a golden phallus. But not
a man's cock. Some other kind, girl dong
or cloud prick or the pointy shadow of the moon
so bright we gasp and say The Sun,
that's where it comes from, that mist is me,

(the sun is the shadow of the moon.
meaning is the shadow of desire.)

That light suffusing mist is thee, pardner,
hot-hipped and sore all about
from Aphrodite's lucidest negotiations.
All flesh wants you because your mind.

A Woman with Flaxen Hair in Norfolk Heard

Wherever you are,
in any season,
I will come to you
from the flowers

she says, and always
call me
by your native language
lest men
think I am strange

or a woman known
only in books,
I am steady as sky
and no further away,

see me in your own
color, my lips
shape the same myths
you live inside,

whenever you do this
I am with you,
to kiss you often to sleep
or wake you
sudden or gentle,
a mouth
in the middle of things.

TONY KITT (Ireland)

A Collage Has a Thousand Mouths

Yes, we knew that cats have a dozen eyes,
but we never heard about matchstick horseracing.
We knew that politicians are cathedrals,
but we've only just learned that mouths prefer
solitary walks.

Go talk to the scissorman,
to sperm flamingos.
Flap your headwings; tell this caterpillar dog
all about leg space.
Hide your target face
among spiderflowers.

Shadow, thy name is symmetry.
Gravity is overstretched.
You may think
a collage is an octogenarian,
but, in fact, it's an octopus.
It hides its ink.

Twenty-Four Heavenly Snippets

Toscanini scanned with AllScan
listens to La Scala glissandi.

Ah, to be drinking again
of this grassland poison!

Clouds
that are also mountains.

The day recites its recipe
into a catkin microphone.

Heaven's Festival Orchestra,
a row of meadowsweet eyes...

To My Real/Imaginary Daughter

In which language do you listen?

Shadows surrounded by doors
    cast a different absence of light.

You have a life now.
I have occasional night flights.

... the weightlessness of a dream...

The vacuity of the past is not contiguous.
Remember the years that looked like nothing?
Do you ever bump into a previous "you"?

You spread the branches of your altitude.
...under the weight of your height...

What ceilings us from growing higher?

Yes, I wrote the flute music
    into this winter.
I wrote my breath too, because we need oxygen
    to observe nothingness.

The conversation's deckled edges...
A weather coalition of colours, voted off
    by the sky...
The finitude of snow...

NOELLE KOCOT (USA)

Ascent of the Mothers

Glorious tripod
Of a million years,

Faces and draft,
Days not uncommon

Where my eye wandered.
Ruined clothes,

Heaps of cars
Over a stray's splayed paws.

I am nothing,
Or else I have made myself

Too big for words.
Take my hands,

There. Now the winter
Light steeps the nerve of it.

The Moon

Elsewhere, the music moves. Did you
Find this road with depth and splash,
Oh from our beds, we must not immolate
Ourselves. The other look you bought,

Time free of hazard, the tower leans into
The rain. We shut the hours as clouds
Surround our heads. A hint of spring
Slides over the sill, as young as time in

The gray February marshes. I have something
To give you, no? And the vines covering
A disgrace amid the maples. A thaw of
What wet sky surrounds, the cries over all

The alarms, our gardens filled with weeds,
The offhand way in which you plunge
In the aproned dusk, what surrounds the
Worms as the moon comes out, their schemes.

Salvation

The long rain, the hungry
Ghost. I am watching something

Fall. The newspaper said
Something leisurely

Today, and I scanned it
Twice to look for your

Image. Nothing's here.
Soon I will no longer be

One big self, and what
Will happen to me? Let go.

Vanity is so yesteryear,
And I am not a fallen hero.

The unglazed windows,
An afterthought out of perspective,

This is what's left,
Something difficult, a fragment.

MICHELE LEGGOTT (New Zealand)

Helix

what can you give me that begins with hinna?
a vision twisting and twisting torch flame or genetic
material from the island of the first morning
a tenderness taking the lyric and turning it inside
out because nothing will ever be the same
a tantrum in the real house of days because some
of them must be picked up and lived despite
a vicissitude oh vicissitudes devouring
the delicate provender of body and soul
a patience on the ladder two steps short
of the full house each keeps for the other
a bed where text is getting around to being
what they want to do today   helix a rich tissue
helix her helix her helix her helix

hyle

the daughters of light, what are their qualities?
I come home from work and there's dinner to fix
I get into bed and it's swing down low goodnight
good morning waking up with you and the story
of my luminous being is lying on the floor
with the rest of the clothes I took off, hidden phases
of the mama I am and you want
to be on top of before the old and holy men ask
how it is the ever-queen distributes sugar grains
to the righteous then makes them clean their teeth
and block the sun with creams before they leave
for school   this you face sweet poet we cannot fall
asleep or in love until you see me through
the unsapphirine unsilvered mirror of where I am

all

out the window on damp wings heady scent
of lilies melisma's little kiss on the dark side
of whatever I was in the barefoot prayer flying over
overflying flown over overflowing coherence
one about the other history and desire objectively
perfect in a temple of particulars ample roma n fleuve
a river novel on the full and just about to close
distances considered immanent but never audible
see we open at a page of choice the stars are out
the words are pure wonder   hyssop hia tus
we breathe calypso phia ls and there's no trouble
distinguishing works and days   we speak
the ties then let them go flying in the places
where love was made and darkness held it close

MICHAEL LEONG (USA)

from "Disorientations"

[NOTE: "Disorientations" collages together—and so "disorients"—two postmodern Orientalist texts: Kent Johnson's Doubled Flowering: From the Notebooks of Araki Yasusada, a yellowface simulation of hibakusha (atomic bomb survivor) literature, and Roland Barthes's Empire of Signs, a semiotic treatise based on an invented system Barthes calls "Japan."]

Here, at the edges
of another
        elsewhere,
we can well understand
that wealth is about
the uninterrupted "ness"
of aboutness,
the way it feeds on the years
when the morning is, all of a sudden,
fresh
        and spattered with *Being*.
You have only to start over again,
but the news articulates
its capitalist diarrhea in crisp characters
that are renewed so rapidly
that it seems everything
is exactly
equal in impetus.
It is not.

      Would you stuff a golden goose
with silver?
Why do you think your parsimony
has been sold back to you
for a "better,"
      more friable reward?
On the contrary,
a subject advances
symbolically,
though out of step,
leading us to the constipated wish
on which all propulsion
depends.
      The modernist time machine
is filled to capacity
or asleep like an eel
or both.
      Exhausted,
it runs on a mouthful of
rice cakes, Zen poetry published
in the United States after 1964,
a faded koan
from Heidegger's notebook,
and the avant-garde faith
that the freshness of water
will be satisfactorily
solidified.

* * *

According to tradition,
      the operation cuts
  but never wounds, slices
 but also coils
    a certain force
      into the oil-glazed fragments
of selection. It is a limited sequence
        of rearrangement, of seamstresses
thinking among surgeons.
    There and then,
this and not that.
            For in order
to be pulled back
     from the forgotten path,
  the thickening movement
must project
      the promised pulsion
of morning.

The world, it was written,
       is a cutting linked
to a pinching together,
     an intricate knot of approximation.
Its tugging still astounds us:
    "it is an index of earth precisely
in the same way that children
     laughing in a ring carry
  a minuscule quantity of salvation."

The child in the American kimono
has the body of a black-bear
    and a mechanical head, the parts of which
we need to grease little by little
        in order for her demeanor to suggest
a modestly happy
    or at least dignified life.
Her long geisha-nails serve
       a deictic function, designating
which visitors
   are to be born
  from the aquatic vessel
of the maternal   before the harmony forks
  into soundless arrows of lineation.

She points at each echo
whispered in brackets.
  Gently swallowing
a donated breath,
     she brings
  into existence
the smallness
  of your half-called name.

* * *

Without looking at his neighbor,
each player releases
a ball of paper
into the vertical hive.
Numerous machines receive it

with the most extreme precision
and propel the ball
through a series of baffles.
Each ball emerges
outside the photograph,
propelled by its own instrumental
lightness of rendezvous.
It is one of the curious
war time customs
to denote that our bearings
mean absolutely nothing
to the pine's indifference,
that the great unknown
has varied clientele.
Like Zen meditation,
it is both collective and solitary—
unless the middle-aged men in the long tunics
start confusing the stupidity of the student
with that of the teacher, in which case
the original teacher/student protocol of 1944
is, at best, unclear. The most important thing
is that the group
plays for the sake of the factory,
with all turnovers going
to the weird whirring
beneath the business suit.
The players know the game has ended
after the dense egg of fat
is somewhat cohesive—
or the urn, placed
imperfectly in the morning parlor,
is full of black rain.

SUSAN LEWIS (USA)

Undeterred

by numbers,
atrophy,

time's slow leak.
This idea stirring

like another birth,
easy to ignore.

The puzzle of
plain speaking,

pain speaking:
what an animal needs,

mother & mate,
maid to order

(in the midst of chaos).
Another energy

sapped. The tree

of life fingering
the space between

desire &
acceptance.

The standard dose
of accommodation,

the standard model
of infliction.

Unexplained gratitude
in the event of interruption.

An amplitude of fear.
Fur stroked,

stricken.
Pitiful cruelty

lashing out in
remorse.

Rattlesnake (Lucky Strike)

That is,
any code you feel

driven to decipher—
these rocks like

stepping stones for
your leggy imagination,

their overbites mouthing
the needy &

the secretive. When
the snow melts, your

opinion of me
rises. Later,

your regard dries up
& I am left with

the hot, dry rocks
& their sibylline,

hot-cold, juiced-
up tenants.

You want me to know
they carry pearls

in their cheeks.
You want me to know

I carry moons
behind my eyes,

like anyone,
like everyone

who wants to tease
vehemence from venom.
Now there are places
I must explore.

There are scales to stroke,
despite the probabilities.

Keyed Out

If you can still
sleep, skip to the

last step &
exercise your

replenished judgment.
If you can't abide

the flighty hours,
rushing & stalling

to spite the war
of pleasure & anxiety,

skip ten steps
past reason.

If you know the difference
between love & out of,

appoint yourself
spiritual leader.

If you agree that
any paradigm serves

as well as any other,
skip to the step marked

kitchen & feed
whoever swallows

what is
offered.

MEDBH McGUCKIAN (Northern Ireland)

Chalice Orchard

It is now, always, the bloodless past,
The wounded present, so unlike the groomed
Groves that do not mind being swept
Away. Every third thought that flounders
In me is dressed in a mist, with a train
Of blue and black moths.

These grandfathered byways are unchanged
As ghosts are, thatching made of wings
Of white birds, wattling of silver.
The translation of the white is rather
The white of flowers that are conditioned,
Perfected by the camber of a wing.

Fields of dreamflowers unnoticed by
The dream me – why do I feel that the
Seven roses require some explanation,
Some further readjustment, some continuation
Of the story? So that eyes may gradually
Become fortified by unvisited gardens.

I have occasional glimpses of imploring
Rose, lying in a room bare except for five
Books, about what is called 'death' –

A vogue, a blossoming, a failure, a few
Stars. It was a sad year, we seem to be
Going on with the old threads

Or it looks threadable by slight
Fingers. Did I call him to me,
Had he come too near, he is waiting
By the icy runway, my hand is wonderfully
Surprised, my hand is in his
Hand, and is my contact with Amen.

It is my lifeblend to write towards
A lessness, I should daydream
In the night as I used to. Then the night
Is cut in half, as afterwards, he had walked
Into me. I have my litany, my minute
Knowledge of sleepless angels.

Encounters with Dust

I avoid books about the present or last war,
The war has never been. The air
Is thinning itself for the breakup of winter.
Breadths of breeze requiring sun
Slice through any and every complaint
To a dark kind of summer.
Moon scuffed at its edges, brighter,
Narrower, smears its self-improvement mirror-
Image of giveaway light into the rich world
At the basement of Europe.

A dull church bell in a parody of greeting
Uses all the languages of the body
To revamp your soul and get that space
Between your thoughts. The day may be
About your spirit, she chimes in with a ribbon
Of praise in your daily gratitude journal,
You find a little spiritual intervention
In your electronic in-box via Skype,
Morsels of frenzy and balm, from those
Electronic churches, before hitting the treadmill.

Remembering the voices that used to fly ahead,
I should have kept both voices alive
In my mouth where shadows fester.
We saw the pale dove-grey coffin,
Overgrown like a stage coffin,
Go down step by step unto the well.
Like hearing the rain in hotels, we dropped

The primroses in at the bottom of a steep,
Brazen grave laid like an old rose,
Surrounded by black and white butterflies.

Roses lit like lamps, it burnt yesterday
With a bunch of our red and white carnations on top
Of it.Its very long after afterglows
Glazed some flicker of the snowdrop
Pallor into the next lap of the year.
There is no way we can make the eyes
Of the blond Christ on his slim cross
Look at us, wrists twinkling with diamonds.
And now some sachet of holy dust
Sets my book alight, in another field.

A Wineskin in the Frost

The floor, if there is one, is a space
Of black words giving out their scent.
The way before the way before
Is a word as common as bitterness.

Like a garden tightening its grip,
The string of her loins threatened to snap,
Bracing her shaking legs and burning knees,
Her swollen, dusky-red feet.

Remember you must leaf the dark-fanged
Rose through the lid of the room, when sorrow
Curdles your foxglove cheeks and the window
Behaviour of the field ends with a river.

Suddenly, I am to have no innerness
Any more: on Holy Saturday, I enter
The rosary. I open it, set it in motion
Till it is closed. Everything that is started

Has to be closed, especially the stillness
Of the rosary, that something was left
Without a proper answer. I was born
In the rosary, time is a rosary,

Each person is a bead, if one suffers,
We suffer too. The chain of belonging
Has no obvious pulse but to live and act
The power of the chant, the power of the number 3.

Not everlook, not ever look, at the raising
Of the most important flagpole, but others'
Hands, one another's mutual perceivings
Upturning the dark to sleep upon a mirror,

Since no-one knows what the past will be
Made of next (snow dying in the lake,
A hood laid on the mountain). I have to
Find my body in his movements

Weighted in places that had no real weight
In them. Propelled out of the sensation
By concepts that did not bend around me,
Walking the length of the field and back.

His body amplifies my hips and the surface
Of my body which is feminine, as if the motion
Were happening to, rather than emerging from,
The body. Undulations from the feet

Cycle up to the torso, I turn into a gentle
Wave, dissolving away from life
Into someone else. My momentum
Was pruned, and the only way I could

Achieve an intentional fall, was to
Become plural, to reassemble, to reform
My own colouring each dawn,
And haunt myself, seeking an outlet.

KB NELSON (Canada)

The Third Turtle

The third turtle stole all the knives
and the whole high hummingday

continued all stay long despite
the boom
      bram kram
           kaslam
of the train track man
despite the hours
        flowers
              flat powers
of the sword envy man

the sun dripped fears
the clouds ripped
    in twos and   fours and
little bitty bits
until the flecks
        flocks
              flacks
flattened over the blue

where I found a room

& you

Trap Kit

And how shall we lay it down tonight

      closely composed reciprocal
          violence perhaps

taut
    force
        wild
tolls

      flash of brass

whirling nylon tips

or shall we caress
    each other with
        thrums   moans
      glimmers
        skin on skin
            click   hush
and the boom boom boom
            as if
                in the next room

how shall we lay it down tonight?

Oregon Coast

wet sand between my toes,
I see the breakers
as a wild woman
deranged by the immense
mass at her back
she pounds her rush her gush
into the cliffs
the dunes
the reefs

her snarled bonnet of salted gray knots,
chaotic halo of flying wisps
blinds her
blinds us all

blasts of sand and brine
season the bitter spikes of beach grass,
armour verbena's bright yellow bouquets,
homogenize bits of kelp, oxygen, crab carapace

a rare smile of lucid sunshine,
a brief burst of sanity
of tranquil hush
makes the power
of her rage
rage
rage
all the more wondrous

as I search the beach
for a channel
to this
will.

CHRIS PRICE (New Zealand)

Stowage

for Jonathan Besser

The sadness of bells sitting silent
shelved like a library of hearts

old salts in their retirement.
Tap one on the lip and a ship

comes ghosting out of the fog
everything passing and human

held in a resonant vessel.
The submarine cathedral

of its ribs still echoes though the ship
is long since flensed and rendered

down – this spare music
the last thing that lingers

the songs of our youth
always the last to go.

Rose and fell

Moist geometry unfurls.
Dawn flushes the birds
from their silence

—hectic petticoats trimmed
with disappearing mist—
and there, under a shaggy hem

of pines, the monster Grendel
stealing home, mouth full
of pinking shears.

His rough palm grips the bruised
root of a plant torn
from a mountainside

releasing scent of a more
legendary bloom.
His pelt

glistens, the girl's words
trapped moths
in his uncomprehending ears.

Wings of flowers
fall and star
the path behind him

as he travels
swiftly over the ground
breathing   breathing.

Swan Song

Imagining transcendence
we pinned the wings
of swans to the blunt
nubs of our shoulder-blades
grafting it on.

Although in time
they grew large enough
to give our bodies levity
our laggard minds
took longer.

Neural runways unrolled
slowly, so at first
we mastered simpler stuff.
It changed the way
we slept. Feather beds

demand too much re-making:
instead we turned
face down, or on our sides
under downy blankets.
Intimacy too required

a whole new repertoire,
but the rustling, infinitely
delicate brush of plumage
made learning joyous.
Yet somewhere on the way

we became a solitary pair
the chill of sadness settling on us
unnoticed at first amid the glorious
warmth of our white cloaks.
We ceased to sing

seeing clearly, from
the vantage of our
airy architecture,
how much there was to mourn for
on the awkward earth.

We took up the endless task
of smoothing ruffled feathers.
Preening, we discovered,
was sublime comfort, but still
it turned us away from the world.

So then we tried to cultivate the art
of listening. Intent:
even the air in our bones
listening, so hard we heard their own high
hollow crack, crystals of river ice

re-forming. Now we grow old, and what
we've heard has ripened slowly
into song: one melancholy burst
to sear the earth
before we're gone.

JON RICCIO (USA)

Visual Field

I transpose letters, the carnival claw's
doldrums as it decides what to negate—

my sentences coin-operated for years.
One doctor thinks dyslexia in the vanity

plate of middle age. I see copse and say
corpse. Another orders an MRI to tell me

why zinnia is ninja, the macula's nasturtium
astray. Sometimes I think pirate patch

and mean eye surgeon, bookmark over
each line like a hydraulic press. White

space self-anagrams, scaffolds an iris.
The test, a dotted screen fit to a vein.

I make more eye contact since my
diagnosis, decades of backstory

wrapped in peanut brittle. Hold
my demons, dynamite your hand.

Disease-iversary with Hall & Oates &

Words, if I haven't seen you in twelve months
there'll be a period of mistaken.
Vaseline, I'll pronounce you vase line.
Companion, champion.
What are relations but tournament?
It's neurology, not lenses, that marks condolence.
The song barreling out of that $8 card?
"Private Eyes Without a Face."
Billy-John-Daryl, how you play
in a Tucson eatery with croutons
spilt into sunflower seeds.
Bride of scotomas,
a slice of vision loss
to stare at each year.
Meringue replaces the maculae
that have literacy by the balls
of my eyes, paperback
rolled into telescope,
syntax mignoned.

The Perspectival We

We anticipate the llama's power-animal ascent. Hence calendars of them in human careers.
    April an optometrist, alpaca toll collector missing the cut.

Weep for the blindfold tailor's death, o un-monogrammed socket.

Wheatfield bench press, pre-intervention Paul Bunyan's anabolic flaunt.

Wheel to library ladder: watch it, you're raining Kenneth Rexroth.

Weaned from astronomy to corona.

Wield a PhD in molecular displacement but careful of houseflies, though Vincent Price makes a good Montreal uncle.

Oui on the Cthulhu tattoo. Kraken my tomfoolery bicep.

Weave it like a tapestry condolence—my neck stubble, your toes—the Hallmark salesman ordered the fabric vendor after months of witticisms on yarnstormers.com.

Weasel basil, roadkill's spice rack.

Weed and without   errand widow.

MATTHEW ROHRER (USA)

Garden of Bees

The narcissus grows past
the towers. Eight gypsy
sisters spread their wings
in the garden. Their gold teeth
are unnerving. Every single
baby is asleep. They want
a little money and I give
them less. I'm charming and
handsome. They take my pen.
I buy the poem from the garden
of bees for one euro. A touch
on the arm. A mystery word.
The sky has two faces.
For reasons unaccountable
my hand trembles.
In Roman times if they were
horrified of bees they kept it secret.

Venus Waning/Apollo Waxing his Car

Then there was the night I decided that if I ignored everyone
I would transcend,

so I covered my ears with my hands,
stepped off the porch and rose like a wet crow

and the sprinklers chattered to each other over the fences.
And "How long will you be gone?" my neighbor called nervously,
my neighbor whose saw I had borrowed,
and "Come down right now!" my landlord called out,
climbing to the roof of his Cadillac to reach me
as he got smaller and smaller.

And there I was with the stars hanging above my house like live wires and the night sky the color of stockings.

I stuck out my tongue to taste the sky
but could not taste.

I inhaled deeply
but could not smell.

I used to look to the sky for comfort
and now there was nothing, not even a seam,
and I looked down and saw that it did not even reach the ground.

And my only company was the satellites counting their sleep
and the Sorrowful Mother swinging her empty dipper in the
    darkness,

the Sorrowful Mother picking her way through the stars over my roof.

And I knew I was nowhere and if I ever took my hands from my ears I would fall.

Childhood Stories

They learned to turn off the gravity in an auditorium
and we all rose into the air,
the same room where they demonstrated
pow-wows and prestidigitation.

But not everyone believed it.
That was the most important lesson
I learned – that a truck driven by a dog
could roll down a hill at dusk
and roll right off a dock into a lake
and sink, and if no one believes you
then what is the point
of telling them wonderful things?

I walked home from the pow-wow
on an early winter night in amazement:
they let me buy the toy tomahawk!
As soon as I got home I was going
to hit my sister with it, but I didn't know this.

JEROME ROTHENBERG (USA)

Coda to a Book of Dreams

For Robert Kelly

*O God, I could be bounded in a nutshell and count myself
a king of infinite space,
were it not that I have bad dreams.*

*No world more clear
than what we see
in dreams
nor more amazing,*
numbers bursting into
stars   & stars
enriching what we learn
when dreaming.

It is no more than this,
to sleep & be
the master of the universe,
not to be bound to earth
but gathering a trillion
other worlds,
to count myself
a little king
stepping aside for time.

Nothing is measured
that the mind can fathom
waking. In the way
her body beckons
when you turn to touch her
coming from a black hole
deep in space
& time. We learn to count
the deeper images
& those still deeper,
gods & angels
dancing on a pin.*   * a chip

Before the dream
turns bad
in which a pin* holds   * a chip
all we know
& all we fear
I stretch out flat
to the Horizon.
I arch above you
like a lid.
I vanish & return.
My name is Death.

The word *extermination*
resonates   nothing
escapes. The world
itself ends in a time
beyond all time
where time ends
leaving a residue behind

of mindless space
& still more mindless
images   the nightmares
that the mind conceals.*   * reveals

To run from time
isn't a choice,
the stars we see
are overwhelming
& block the view
or bring up images
of light & dark,
a flickering
across the map
of time,
the flow of sand
in dreams.

"To Dream Infinity"

1/
To dream
infinity
& know the time
draws nigh
never more near
than now

2/
the far look
of an ancient
god
his hands
ready to bring us
down

3/
there is
no end to it
the universe
escapes us
& another universe
takes shape

4/
open & shut
absent
a god
whose malice
holds us
too close

5/
still to be
free & clear
the deeper
image
out of our beck
& call

6/
seeing the others
fallen
entering the pitch
& blackness
figments of an endless
mindless world

7/
the beauty
of the never-
ending
freezes us
more spectral
than a dream

8/
how many circles
make up a universe
if only the eye
allows it?
nothing that the mind
can know or tell

one
two
three
four
five
wild circles

From "In the Shadow of a Mad King"

A Work in Progress

"faces"

(1)
a family of thieves
& freaky princes
how they surround a mad king
keeping the faces of the dying
out of sight

(2)
no room for shame
the mad king stares
at his own face
the dead like hornets fly around
& won't be still

(3)
shadows crowd his mind
& leave a mad king
pining for a vanished throng
faces he no longer sees
only in dreams

(4)
When all is lost a mad king
cannot find himself
looking for a way to track his face

the outline of his shadow
disappearing

(5)
A circle of believers
holds out hands to touch
a mad king
never a touch enough
to show his face

(6)
a mad king hides the deaths of millions
the fragments of a mirror
that multiplies his face a million times
sending his faces hurtling
into mindless space

JAKE SHEFF (USA)

Creosote Covenant

The fire truck is not the frotteurism dismantled by
parents to replicate on a rhizome-and-blues disc,
is not the satellite of Seattle's intended
nor a combination of gruesome celerity
and menarche without monocle or manacle,
but the implements are in place to rectify what-
ever, like some incorrect celery, comes our way.

None of this is writ on the to-do list of my cat
or any other legitimately enzymat-
ic grown up. It isn't carved, like some accusation,
in a heart with an arrow on some sturgeon or fir.
But whenever my wife's unheralded look of *You
turn on me, you turn me on* appears, it dwarfs all fires.

Emerson's Submarine

Backward fish of outer reaches,
contemplating air; reacting to
destiny's immersion in your aches:
you're not my problem. A grungy
sky attacks suburban difficulties?
The grainy aftermaths of noon?
Pour me Kentucky bourbon. Pour
another dead person's name,
playing hooky, buried in Pilot
Knob. The sun's scurrilous
on boiling waves, but cichlids
make nice with squirrels then.
Like ads for more life, the good
master adds depth above the
surface. Winnowing semblances
of minnows emanate below.

Why Tamper with the Spectral Spoil?

The string was hung above the ground –
31" long and 31" high. Below,
The compost pile, and under that
A primum non nocere agreement
Between the celibate intensity and
Verruciform, bantam network. (My skin
Like microfiche, this property
Anathema to lithium, Athena, random
Miracles.) The seven 1s and seven 0s
Ran above: retaliation's form of libel;
The postal industry's falsetto trait in mime.

The ground's gung-ho astringent, like a
13, cinches the quotidian by its one-and-thirty
Piles of short-and-curlies; and under,
Nociceptors: agriculture's double-ply
Phenomena, in tandem with celebrity
Intestines; the skein of net worth cruciform.
(The micro-cliché improperly ties
Lythrum to the enemy, the anthem in the killer
Mirror's ransom.) The seven 1s and seven 0s
Farm retaliation, run aground these billet-
Doux encrusted mines of tried and true.

JULIA STAKHIVSKA (Ukraine)

Coastline

Everyone can see the victims rising from the bottom
of their faces.
The parents' submarines are stained with silt;
they have mussel-like eyes and rusty eyebrows.

The coastline ... a dream ... the edge of foam
moves up the rocks and falls down suddenly
along an embarrassingly straight line.

And then reality begins to resemble
a locked greenhouse
where one can grow the vine of suffering
in an old porcelain pot;

where magnificent peacocks of sorrow
strut into the harbours of hands and the wrists
of rivers, and a smile betrays itself like a bow
that launches a playful arrow.

Tender Is the Night

The night is lined with yellow lantern satin.
The lanterns have replaced old trees, and now
one might think this is their afterlife:
distilling juices of electric currents,
occasionally creaking and gathering together local ants,
throwing themselves against our green window-panes
at full speed, like phosphoric hornets,
and then dropping onto the sills, barely alive.
At night all the bodies tighten up and grow nacre,
so they can hide in their shells, their little coffins.
The day resembles shallow water,
with turtle shields in the sand.

Orpheus

Dawn sand gets into my eyes, and I can't figure out
whether the hill of a heel is real or it is
the white llama of a leg that flashes in the distance.

Orpheus convenes the creatures as best he can:
sometimes with the blues—
so much water saturates his sounds—
sometimes with a shining metallic blade,
and then moles burrow further:
there's such a powerful force in this depth!

Let each of us be the one whose heart he owns,
we heard one fine afternoon
when a fox admired its sly fur coat
and a mouse shook like a jelly bean.

And now he is sitting like a lost soul
overwhelmed with the weight of the hearts
inside him, stones in the stream.

Translated from the Ukrainian by Anatoly Kudryavitsky

THOMAS TOWNSLEY (USA)

A Month of Thursdays

A month of Thursdays I waited, nibbled by hedge hogs
of regret. A month of Thursdays, my eyes gouged
by real crows who spoke to me so I would not
feel alone; they said "This is the whitening, the
cleansing of matter." "Then why is it so dark?"
I asked, for I had no understanding. A month
of Thursdays, a cyclops's eye. A month of Thursdays,
a razor blade's reminiscences, an eel's sense of purpose,
a hot pavement strewn with starfish like cookies on a tray.
The turning wheel evokes a sound of bells. A month of
Thursdays, and no mention of the diadem. Does the night
have teeth? Are there voices in the well? I'm clutching
father's war medals, through which the radio signals come.
A month of Thursdays, time's barbed wire around my throat,
lungs turned to pumice. "We've brought you company,"
say the crows. "His name is Paracelsus. He will explain
everything." But all he does is spit in my ear. This restores my
vision, but it's not the same because the memory of
darkness overlays everything, save that which is holy,
and there's nothing I can do about it.

Tangent of Ardency

Beside a house with liver spots,
near the coughing lilacs, flows a brook
that turns the calendar's pages and
bears away flotsam shaped
like tiny hats.

"Where are the lovers?" it seems to ask.

In the wooded glen nearby, the lovers crouch
amidst allegorical figures who declare
their relationship to Fate, using the
language of antiquity.

The lovers are ignorant of this language.
Beside them bubbles a spring, the brook's source,
with its tale of loaves and fishes,
of many from one.

From here, one can see pinecones dropping.
One can dine on the meat of the sky,
which replenishes itself like
tankards of ale for rich men.

From here, one cannot see the obsidian threads,
nor feel the disbursements. One cannot taste
the imploding compass. Here, it is said,
one never waits but always remains.

Accordion-Playing Clam

To make a clam play an accordion is to invent—
not to discover.
—Wallace Stevens

What are the parts of a pier? Planks and pilings?
Shall I risk my life for a poem? My dog eats snow
and leaves his water bowl untended. How thengt
shall I weigh shame? By the clam's beard I'll know thee,
by its "Lady of Spain" I'll measure this song,
though seabirds lack color and the waves' paraphrase
misquotes, endlessly misquotes, things as they are.
Once, I lived with gypsies; they gave me a secret name
without purpose, like a rosary seen through a crystal ball,
like invisible cuff-links. I use an adder's fang
for a hat-pin, for all the good it does.
Refrigerators humming Mozart, cotton fields of
white regret, the e pluribus Unum of doorbells in childhood,
arcane musings of Egyptologists at the Fratricide symposium—
these and more shall grace thy song.
What are the parts of reality that they might
be discovered at a Sunday morning's tea or at this clam recital?
The most colorful birds dwell inland, along emerald rivers.
Their drowsy songs breathe false fire; though it light
a thousand nights, it will not burn.

MARC VINCENZ (USA)

Wheels of Industry

Light turns blue, turns old.
The gears and cogs roar.

Nailed to clouds,
the dying float above.

Drained, we emerge
from stained glass

among the trees
raising arms, singing.

As the dust rises
the sky falls and the grain

nestles in our pockets.

On a Scale of One to Fish

O to be desired, and to be desired back so easily.

Yes, I know the timpani rolls.

The crashing cymbals of reality.

We were jaded in the scale, just above where the fleshy part dwells, or perhaps, on another scale, we had found the best flesh.

A sunrise always helps.

Riptide

Squared away.
Floored in wooden clogs.

What nibbles?

See that signpost over there?
That's all he can do.
He sits on the ice perched over his small fish.

He knows who's biting
And waits alone.

LES WICKS (Australia)

An Edge of Our Plan Covenant

This beach is not dreaming.

It writes with an algal care
then loses control in high tide.
Dark gas, poisoned walls
nothing better than barefoot.

Minor leakage in the corners of a boy,
the weight of his hair
that hangs like an exhausted mango tree.

Beneath the ropes of surf
sand
Everywhere.

When fingers open they grab blindly.
Each heart is a crater
the breast & arm
A moment, please
Shatter my back like a rock
on the available space
that is your love.

Deeper isn't purity.
Fifth, granular.
We are difficult situations.

Milk Beach

Prayer is this discard basketball
washed up at the shoreline.

The poem is inside that ball,
 air under pressure.

Tears require practice.

We are wrapped in poisonous bandages of summer.
As always
the cure is the punishment.
We build up   fall down
so can't be just flesh
though probably less
than the sum of our garbage.

All this beneath
a sniggering fig –
my list of miseries
is still just a sheet of paper
even my fingers keep saying
just like this.

No fish lose sleep over Justice.
They are their own comfort, connection & cloister.
Beneath the call of muezzin ferries
each basketball is beached
in its very own moment.

Mea Culpa

Today is full of no direction.
Rarely has been or perhaps
just impassable routes for me.
So stepped outside the honeycomb —
the air's so hard but
I hold on.
You can hug something long enough,
it becomes a simulacrum of loving & reprieve.

Pinned on the plateau of a nagging mortality
my breath is seized by hungry owls.
They dissect with a holy patience
until the bones of words clatter downtrack to
what used to be safety.

There was a book on bodies that I never read
(though am a co-author).
The fuss all dissipated
after lies were exposed.
I am richer now.

JOSHUA MARIE WILKINSON (USA)

Poem for Mathias Svalina

Here is where the dead go
to get noisy tromping out
songs to glove through
collating the meat with giant
hooks. Says the night
wants from us what the night
cannot do for itself until
the lantern's shaky song
gets twisted out. Copy lengthwise,
elliptical star votive &
methods for boat wrecking
crews of this known only
for callused laughter,
crippled star of bees.
Socket say sorry but you might not
live this night through. So say it.
City get us back with your wrong
cuts. Even some of the missteps
are better than the so-called up
audial now.

Poem for Brandon Shimoda

Lavender smock of spotted light & clam shovels
for the dirge to gather us out. Well, you found
what you couldn't've come for
& it keeps finding itself in your own
messages—crow lines to carry the voice
of the poem back home, home here,
now undoable nets of the past. I can
see your thread. Your thread is
not invisible. My grandmother is
in San Francisco and it's 1944.
Oppen's brick, all the days go off
like wheat. Lice. Fruitrot.
Can I say I hear it and still mean
I'm not coming? You go through it
with the reparation smudged out.
You laugh like a fire. Pines.
Ice boots. Gossip to rinse your
wrists with. Wetter than the moon
in Stanford's poems, well, no. But
you sing listening throughout.

Poem for Laynie Browne

I guess conceptualism
woke up in the sad nets of yore
& you made another space
to counter it—not

in the armchair of the scoffer,
let alone corroborator but
as an act—more renewal
& recombinatory, quadrupling
the crazed space of
what the edge of making
might could look like if it did
some quality asking together
to gather.

JEFFREY CYPHERS WRIGHT (USA)

Topol Management Company

Often in the lonesome section
I barbeque the mirror. Your laughter
an elixir. Where sometimes means
X and never means Y. There

we cross hairs in our new direction.
Eating the bones of dreams, we
both have grown fatter but now
is notorious and the speaker's patter

makes no sense although I discern
a pattern of adaption. Currently
half past to die for.
Waiting for the number one train.

Changing Station

Agony—the inevitability of our demise.
We were spinning sugar when the giant
crutch fell short. The clocks running
for their lives. The city humming
like a freezer. A black caboose on ice.

You were making mushroom ragu.
I was admiring your industry, reading
the Metropolitan section. When
the denouement comes, look for me
in the cockpit handing out straws
to clutch at as we veer into a viral spiral.

The Empire State Building's opal spire
cuts into night. That's kinda how
I am now—a lightsaber, ready for hire.

Temporary Sanity

> *forever in the sweat of fire.*
> —Philip Lamantia

Winter's white heart steams.
Venus pins night to the sky.
A few stars are hung out to dry.

On call at the dream hospital,
my gang of bells rings.

Me and you in the pitch light,
throb like a pulsar.
Listen. Your canals can hear
my eyelids beating time
into wings of gold foil.

All of what I say to you comes
with a moneyback guarantee.

And snow only really talks
when it starts to melt.

PALOMA YANNAKAKIS (USA)

To Touch Blood On Stone

I readied myself in the rain.

How much forgetting it takes
   to remember, your mouth

now curving around
 a question incinerated
   at the root. Hold it

close to the hilt, the mandrake's
 shriek when it's torn from the ground
   for good. I waited

a long time to hear the echo
 descend in diminished stops,
   through rooms too numerous to count.

The bird in movement goes on
   forever landing.

Journal of Discontent (1)

In the dwelling of the outermost rock,
with my one good body
and bone-picked soul I flung
across the ground to see if it would
support the idle weight of my ideas,
listing. Less the loss

but still on the registry,
a faint numeral for reckoning.
Hid beneath a strip of selvage that should
have been mine discarded
on display in the raw tangle that began
to resemble
a distant association of bones.

Surely they won't undertake me
in the crosswind
without a care to my name, no
wherewithal, I said. The dense netting heaves over
flanked by two perfectly brown horses.

Tell me where it ends,
and if it's true. Escape and evasion.
As when something indescribable hooks
into being.

Journal of Discontent (2)

I slept in the shadow of my waking
the curve of its ash branched
into morning tremor, jay
that jangled. Galloping across my chest
the many-stranded cough, incipient wave.

Wings shadow wings
on the window frame,
flashing tips
landing on the clapboard outside.

When it was no longer possible to pretend
we would escape unscathed, to move an inch
meant the world.

The ground cut away,
sash of remembrance roped to
some forgotten tree at the edge of a
public square.

JOHN YAU (USA)

A Sheaf of Pleasant Voices

There are rooftops
made of cloud remnants

gathered by a trader
dabbling in car parts and burlap

At night, I dive onto the breeze
fermenting above the dirt

and dream that I am a crocodile
a tin of shoe polish, an audience of two

In the morning, before the smallest yawn
becomes a noodle, I am offered

a ribbon of yellow smoke
I opt for fuzzy rocks and clawed water

and, of course, the perishable window
I am one of the last computer

chain errors to be illuminated
I tell you there are rooftops

on which the moon stops
being a cold jewel

And one by one the mountains
begin their descent from

the chambers of a lost book

I Heard A Man Say

My genitals aren't worth listening to
Chinatown smells like brown cheese

wrapped in sweltering fish
Old men still spit on sidewalks

while smoking cigarettes
next to bandaged sprinkler systems

Obesity is the name you sat down with
It's never going to let you up

This could have happened anywhere
It's time to retire that smiling potato

No tomorrow to hang your hat on
When did happiness get so chewy

You have officially become an event
You look like you want to end up in a trash bag

Sky full of half-bitten stars
are we a sack of crumbs falling from a
       catastrophe

I used to date a mannequin in a space suit
Whenever I look out the porthole

I can see the planet that ejected me
Is it because I am too human

or not quite human enough
Time to turn in old frequencies

Join other raincoats in a painting

First Language Lesson

As you may have inferred, Ka Pow is not a spicy chicken dish
Meanwhile, you are an accident waiting to repurpose yourself

Who are you to mix up languages? This is not a smorgasbord
You have to remember that you are a cylinder, a form of fodder

Meanwhile, you are an accident waiting to repurpose yourself
Why do you need an expensive phone? It won't help you in the future

You have to remember that you are a cylinder, a form of fodder
Our company motto: other than you, no waste shall go to waste

Why do you need an expensive phone? It won't help you in the future
Have you ever thought of joining the circus? You might find a home there

Our company motto: other than you, no waste shall go to waste
Choosing suitable punishments is an unavoidable necessity

Have you ever thought of joining the circus? You might find a home there.
If you are speaking about my place in the universe, that's not right

Choosing suitable punishments is an unavoidable necessity
Hasn't the sky repeatedly proven to be the most excellent manager

If you are speaking about my place in the universe, that's not right
Memories are iridescent insects iniltrating your dreams

Hasn't the sky repeatedly proven to be the most excellent manager
Little sphinxes, I have instructed you to the best of my ability

Memories are iridescent insects infiltrating your dreams
As you may have inferred, Ka Pow is not a spicy chicken dish

Little sphinxes, I have instructed you to the best of my ability
Who are you to mix up languages? This is not a smorgasbord

ANDREW ZAWACKI (USA)

Collider

Verona inside
the body, the
veins, & Venice
dissolved in the mind,
spooling at speeds
of incommensurate order:
a bullet
train crossing a backgammon
board, or the metro
to fit inside a metro
-nome: help me,
someone says,
take off my face

Any Other Eviction, Than The Frequent

If it be warfare, let it be mistress
and midnight up that slope,
not reticent in a weather
of withdrawal, its salmon-roe tint,
the shabby grass it grazes

but varnished to richterline
under a prismatic glare:
delinquent churn of cloudswath
and gust, calving a foreshore filth
from its respiratory lunge:

inlaid verges blear kaleidoscopic,
larkspur and loosestrife splinter
and render afire, as frontiers to scour
or confiscate, and laving dark
these latent, these restive affronts:

I was in love with a river
and its recoil - water and whither
it went is a doctrine of veil,
applique to what angle of incident
little, what lightless, unhinge.

Credo

You say wind is only wind
& carries nothing nervous
in its teeth.
    I do not believe it.

I have seen leaves desist
        from moving
although the branches
        move, & I
believe a cyclone has secrets
the weather is ignorant of.
        I believe
in the violence of not knowing.

I've seen a river lose its course
& join itself again,
        watched it court
a stream & coax the stream
into its current,

        & I have seen
rivers, not unlike
        you, that failed to find
their way back.

        I believe the rapport
between water & sand, the advent
from mirror to face.

    I believe in rain
to cover what mourns,
     in hail that revives
& sleet that erodes, believe
whatever falls
   is a figure of rain

& now I believe in torrents that take
everything down with them.

The sky calls it quits,
    or so I believe,
when air, or earth, or air
has had enough.

   I believe in disquiet,
the pressure it plies, believe a cloud
to govern the limits of night.

    I say I,
but little is left to say it, much less
mean it—
  & yet I do.

    Let there be
no mistake:
 I do not believe
things are reborn in fire.
They're consumed by fire

& the fire has a life of its own.

Biographical Notes

Will Alexander was born in Los Angeles, California, in 1948. He received a BA from the University of California–Los Angeles in 1972. Alexander published his first poetry collection, *Vertical Rainbow Climber* (Jazz Press), in 1987. He went on to publish numerous books of poetry, including *Kaleidoscopic Omniscience* (Skylight Press, 2013), *The Sri Lankan Loxodrome* (New Directions, 2009), and *Asia & Haiti* (Sun & Moon Press, 2000). He has taught at several universities, including the Jack Kerouac School of Disembodied Poetics and the University of California–San Diego. Alexander is the recipient of a California Arts Council Fellowship, a PEN/Oakland Josephine Miles Award, and a Whiting Fellowship, among many others. He lives in California.

John Thomas Allen is from New York. His latest book entitled *Lumière* was published by NightBallet Press in 2014. His poems have appeared in *Veil: a Journal of Dark Musings, Arsenic Lobster Magazine, Sulfur, Mad Verse, The Cimarron Review*, etc., and he has a story in the anthology titled *Narrow Doors in Wide Green Fields* edited by R.W. Spryszak. He edited the anthology of Surrealist poetry entitled *Nouveau's Midnight Sun: Transcriptions from Golgonooza and Beyond* (Ravenna Press, 2014). In 2019, he won James Tate Prize for his chapbook entitled *Rolling in the Third Eye* (SurVision Books, 2020).

Clayre Benzadón is a University of Miami MFA graduate student alumni and graduate of Brandeis University. Her chapbook, *Liminal Zenith*, was published by SurVision Books in 2019. She is formerly the editor of *Sinking City* magazine and currently a poetry reader for *Split Lip Magazine* and Broadsided Press's Instagram editor. She has been published by *The Acentos Review, HerStory, Rat's Ass Review, Poetry Breakfast, Fairy Tale Review, Hobart, MudRoom Magazine, Kissing Dynamite, SurVision*, etc. She was awarded the 2019 Alfred Boas Poetry Prize for her sequence entitled "Linguistic Rewilding".

Lee Ballentine is a retired book publishing CEO, software engineer, veteran of 1970s/1980s start-ups and art detective. He edited the journal of new surrealism and found photography, *UR-VOX*, and the anthology *POLY: New Speculative Writing* (Ocean View Books, 1989). Lee Ballentine is the author of eight poetry collections, including *Phase Language* (Pantograph Press, 1995).

Charles Borkhuis is a poet, playwright, and essayist living in New York City. He has published seven collections; the most recent is entitled *Dead Ringer* (BlazeVOX Books, 2016). Among his other collections are *Disappearing Act* (Wave Books, 2014), *Savoir-Fear* (Spuyten Duyvil, 2003) and *Alpha Ruins*, which was selected by Fanny Howe as runner-up for the William Carlos Williams 2001 Book Award. Two of his essays on innovative American poetry were recently published in separate anthologies *Telling It Slant* and *We Who Love to Be Astonished* (University of Alabama Press).

Lily Brown was born in Boston, Massachusetts, and currently lives with her family in Maine. She is author of the poetry collection *Rust or Go Missing* (Cleveland State University Poetry Center, 2011) and five chapbooks, including *The Haptic Cold* (Ugly Duckling Presse, 2013). Her poetry has appeared in journals such as *A Public Space*, *Mississippi Review*, *Lana Turner*, *Typo*, *American Letters and Commentary*, and *Colorado Review*.

Garrett Caples lives in San Francisco. He is the author of *Lovers of Today* (2021), *Power Ballads* (2016), *Retrievals* (2014), *Quintessence of the Minor: Symbolist Poetry in English* (2010), *Complications* (2007), and *The Garrett Caples Reader* (1999). He is an editor at City Lights Books, where he curates the Spotlight poetry series. Caples was also a contributing writer to the *San Francisco Bay Guardian* and has co-edited the *Collected Poems of Philip Lamantia* (2013), *Particulars of Place* (2015) by Richard O. Moore, and *Incidents of Travel in Poetry: New and Selected Poems* (2016) by Frank Lima.

Angela Cleland was born in Inverness, Scotland, and grew up in Dingwall by the Cromarty Firth. A poet and novelist, she won the Templar Poetry Pamphlet and Collection Competition in 2006 and published the pamphlet *Waiting to Burn* (Templar Poetry, 2006) and a full collection *And in Here the Menagerie* (Templar Poetry, 2007) as a result. *Room of Thieves* (Salt, 2013) followed. Her latest collection of poetry is *Real Cute Danger* published by Broken Sleep Books in 2022.

Andrei Codrescu was born in Romania in 1946, and moved to Detroit in 1966. In 1983 Codrescu founded *Exquisite Corpse: A Journal of Books & Ideas*. He has edited several annual anthologies of work from the journal, as well as the anthologies *American Poets Say Goodbye to the 20th Century* (1996) and *American Poetry Since 1970: Up Late* (1996). Trying his hand in multiple genres, Codrescu has authored nonfiction and memoirs, and directed a documentary film, for which he won the Peabody Award. He is the author of dozens of books of poetry, including *Jealous Witness* (2008), *It Was Today* (2003), and his debut, *License to Carry a Gun* (1970), which won the Big Table Poetry Award. He is also the recipient of the 2005 Ovidius Prize.

Alison Dunhill lives in Norfolk, England. A visual artist and an art historian, she has had poems published in *Joe Soap's Canoe*, *SurVision Magazine*, *The Fenland Poetry Journal*, and in *Contemporary Surrealist and Magic Realist Poetry* anthology (ed. by Jonas Zdanys, Lamar University Press, 2022). She also had two pieces longlisted for the Fish Flash Fiction Prize in 2020. Her first poetry pamphlet, "Gig Soup Scoop", was published by Trans Gravity Advertiser in 1972. Her second chapbook, *As Pure as Coal Dust,* won the James Tate Prize and was published by SurVIsion Books in 2021. Her MPhil thesis forges links between interwar surrealism and 1970s US photography.

John Godfrey was born in Massena, New York. He has lived in the East Village since the 1960s and taught at the Poetry Project in 1974-1975 and 1982-1983. He is the author of more than a dozen collections of poetry, including *26 Poems* (1971), *The Music of the Curbs* (1976), *Push the Mule* (2001), *City of Corners* (2008), *Tiny Gold Dress* (2012), and *The City Keeps: Selected and New Poems 1966-2014* (2016).

Philip Hammial is an Australian poet, with 30 poetry collections published. He was educated at Central Michigan University. His poems have appeared in 31 poetry anthologies (in seven countries) & in 120 journals in fifteen countries. He has represented Australia at fourteen international poetry festivals, most recently at Poetry Africa 2016 in

Durban, SA. In 2009/10 he was the Australian writer-in-residence for six months at the Cité International des Arts in Paris.

Roberto Harrison was born in Oregon. A poet, essayist, and visual artist, he is the author of poetry collections titled *Os* (subpress, 2006), *Counter Daemons* (Litmus Press, 2006), *bicycle* (Noemi Press, 2015), *culebra* (Green Lantern Press, 2016), *Bridge of the World* (Litmus, 2017), *Yaviza* (Atelos, 2017), as well as of many chapbooks, including *Bridge of the World* (cannot exist, 2011). With Andrew Levy he published and edited *Crayon* magazine from 1997 to 2008. He currently publishes and edits The Bronze Skull Press chapbook series. He lives in Milwaukee with his wife, the poet Brenda Cárdenas.

Nicholas Alexander Hayes is based in Chicago, Illinois. He is the author of *Ante-Animots: Idioms and Tales*, NIV: 39 & 7 (both published by BlazeVOX), *Between* (Atropos), *Third SexPot* (Beard of Bees), and Metastaesthetics (Atropos). His work has been featured in the anthologies *Madder Love: Queer Men and the Precincts of Surrealism, Quantum Genre in the Planet of Arts,* and in *Contemporary Surrealist and Magic Realist Poetry* anthology (ed. by Jonas Zdanys, Lamar University Press, 2022). His poems also appear in *Scab, Peculiar Mormyrid, SurVision,* and *BlazeVox Journal.*

Stefania Heim was raised in Queens, NY. She is an associate professor of English at Western Washington University. A former poetry editor at *Boston Review,* she is also a founding editor of *Circumference: Poetry in Translation* and the author of the poetry collections *Hour Book* (Ahsahta Press, 2018) and *A Table That Goes On for Miles* (Switchback Books, 2014), as well as the translator of *Geometry of Shadows*: the Italian poems of Giorgio de Chirico (A Public Space Books, 2019). Her translation of de Chirico's novel, *Mr. Dudron*, will be published by A Public Space Books in 2024.

Bob Heman is living on Long Island (NYC). His most recent publications are *The House of Grand Farewells* (Luna Bisonte Prods, 2018), *The Number 5 is Always Suspect* (Presa Press, 2019), a collection of collaborations with Cindy Hochman, and *Cone Transformed* (Poets Wear Prada, 2021. His poems and collages appear in *New American*

Writing, Caliban Online, Otoliths, Indefinite Space, Home Planet News online, and *NOON: journal of the short poem,* and in *Contemporary Surrealist and Magic Realist Poetry* anthology (ed. by Jonas Zdanys, Lamar University Press, 2022). Since 1972 he has edited CLWN WR (formerly Clown War).

Helen Ivory was born in 1969 in Luton, England, and has lived in Norwich since 1990. A poet and visual artist, she has won a Gregory Award from the Society of Authors and has published five collections with Bloodaxe Books, including *The Double Life of Clocks (2002), The Dog in the Sky (2006), The Breakfast Machine (2010), Waiting for Bluebeard (2013;* short-listed for the East Anglian Book Awards in 2014), and *The Anatomical Venus* (2019). She edits the webzine *Ink Sweat and Tears,* and is tutor and Course Director for the UEA/Writers Centre Norwich online creative writing programme. *Fool's World* a collaborative Tarot with the artist Tom de Freston (Gatehouse Press) won the 2016 Saboteur Award for Best Collaborative Work. *Hear What the Moon Told Me,* book of collage/ mixed media/ acrylic painted poems, was published in 2016 by Knives Forks and Spoons Press. SurVision books published her chapbook, *Maps of the Abandoned City,* in 2019.

Andrew Joron was born in San Antonio and raised in Germany, Massachusetts, and Montana. He is an assistant professor of creative writing at San Francisco State University and the author of several collections of poetry, including *The Absolute Letter* (Flood Editions, 2018), *Trance Archive: New and Selected Poems* (2010), *Fathom* (2003), and *Science Fiction* (1992). He is also the author of *The Cry at Zero: Selected Prose* (2007) and *Neo-Surrealism; Or, The Sun at Night: Transformations of Surrealism in American Poetry* (2004). His poetry has also been included in the anthologies *American Hybrid* (2009) and *Primary Trouble* (1996). His translations from the German include surrealist Richard Anders' *The Footsteps of One Who Has Not Stepped Forth* (1999) and philosopher Ernst Bloch's *Literary Essays* (1998).

George Kalamaras was born in 1956 in Chicago and grew up in Indiana He holds a doctorate in English from State University of New

York at Albany. He has published eight books of poetry including *Kingdom of Throat-Stuck Luck* (Elixir Press, 2012), *The Recumbent Galaxy* (C&R Press, 2010), co-authored with Alvaro Cardona-Hine, *Gold Carp Jack Fruit Mirrors* (Bitter Oleander Press, 2008) and *The Theory and Function of Mangoes* (Four Way Books, 2000). He has also published seven poetry chapbooks and more than 950 poems in anthologies and magazines in the USA and abroad. Former Poet Laureate of Indiana (2014-2016), he is Professor of English at Indiana University-Purdue University Fort Wayne, where he has taught since 1990.

Charles Kell is an assistant professor at the Community College of Rhode Island and editor of the *Ocean State Review*. He is the author of *Cage of Lit Glass*, chosen by Kimiko Hahn for the 2018 Autumn House Press Poetry Prize. Recent work appears in *The Brooklyn Review*, *Laurel Review*, and *Hobart*. In 2021, SurVision Books published his chapbook, *Pierre Mask,* that won the James Tate Poetry Prize.

Robert Kelly was born in Brooklyn, N.Y. in 1935 and educated at the City University of New York and Columbia University. A poet associated with the Deep Image group, he is Professor of Literature at Bard College, N.Y. He published more than 50 collections of poetry and prose, the latest being *Leaflight* (Metambesen, 2020). In 1991, he was the recipient of the American Book Award, and his poems have been translated into many languages. He was the 2016-2017 Poet Laureate of Dutchess County, New York.

Tony Kitt is from Dublin, Ireland. A former teacher of creative writing, he has been an editor for SurVision Books since 2022. His poetry collection entitled *Endurable Infinity* has been published in 2022 by University of Pittsburgh Press, in the Pitt Series. His other collection, *Sky Sailing*, is due from Salmon Poetry in 2024. His poetry chapbooks are *The Magic Phlute* (2019) and *Further through Time* (2022). His poems also appear in many magazines and anthologies, including the *Contemporary Surrealist and Magic Realist Poetry* anthology (ed. by Jonas Zdanys, Lamar University Press, 2022). He edited the anthology entitled *Invasion: Ukrainian Poems about the War* (SurVision Books, 2022) and was the winner of Maria Edgeworth Poetry Prize.

Noelle Kocot was born in Brooklyn, New York, and raised there. She is the author of nine collections of poetry, including *Ascent of the Mothers (Wave Books, 2022), Phantom Pains of Madness* (Wave Books, May 2016), *Soul in Space* (Wave Books, 2013), *The Bigger World* (Wave Books, 2011), and a book of translations of some of the poems of Tristan Corbière, *Poet by Default* (Wave Books, 2011). She currently teaches at The New School and lives in New Jersey. She is the recipient of awards from the National Endowment for the Arts, the Academy of American Poets, The Fund for Poetry and the *American Poetry Review*. She is the current Poet Laureate of Pemberton Borough, New Jersey.

Michele Leggott is from New Zealand. She was educated in the UK and Canada. She teaches at the University of Auckland. She has published four collections of poetry, including *DIA,* which won the 1995 New Zealand Book Award for Poetry, and *Vanishing Points* (2017), both published by Auckland University Press. Her other book is *Reading Zukofsky's '80 Flowers'* (Johns Hopkins, 1989). In 1991–92, she was the poetry editor of *Landfall.* She also co-edited *Opening the Book: New Essays on New Zealand Writing* (Auckland UP, 1995).

Michael Leong lives in Ohio. He is Robert P. Hubbard Assistant Professor of Poetry at Kenyon College. His most recent books are *Words on Edge* (Black Square Editions, 2018), *Contested Records: The Turn to Documents in Contemporary North American Poetry* (University of Iowa Press, 2020), and *Sky-Quake: Tremor of Heaven* (co•im•press, 2020) a co-translation, with Ignacio Infante, of Vicente Huidobro's operatic long poem. His poems also appear in many magazines and anthologies, including *Contemporary Surrealist and Magic Realist Poetry* anthology (ed. by Jonas Zdanys, Lamar University Press, 2022).

Susan Lewis lives in New York City and edits *Posit* magazine. She is the author of *Zoom,* (The Word Works, 2018; winner of the Washington Prize), *Heisenberg's Salon* (BlazeVOX, 2017), *This Visit* (BlazeVOX, 2014), *How to Be Another* (Cervena Barva Press, 2013), *State of the Union* (Spuyten Duyvil, 2013), and a number of chapbooks, including

Commodity Fetishism, winner of the Cervena Barva Press Chapbook Prize. Her poetry has appeared in many journals & anthologies, including *Agni, Berkeley Poetry Review, Boston Review, The Brooklyn Rail, Cimarron, Conjunctions, Diode, Interim, New American Writing, The New Orleans Review, Seneca Review,* and *VOLT.* She is the founder and Editor-in-chief of *Posit* (positjournal.com).

Medbh McGuckian was born in Belfast. Educated at Queen's University, Belfast, she worked as writer-in-residence and taught English at the same university. Among her poetry collections are *The Flower Master* (1982), *Venus and the Rain* (1984), *On Ballycastle Beach* (1988), *Marconi's Cottage* (1991), *Captain Lavender* (1995), *Shelmalier* (1998), *The Face of the Earth.* She won the Poetry Society Competition, an Eric Gregory Award, the Cheltenham Award, the Rooney Prize, the Irish Funds' Literary Award and the Alice Hunt Bartlett Award.

KB Nelson is from Canada. A graduate of Simon Fraser University's Southbank writing program, she has lived in Ontario, Yukon, Alberta, New Brunswick and New Zealand, and is now based in Greater Vancouver. She writes poetry and short fiction, and has won awards in both. Her haiku have appeared in Icebox, her poems in SurVision, as well as in local anthologies and in *Contemporary Surrealist and Magic Realist Poetry* anthology (ed. by Jonas Zdanys, Lamar University Press, 2022). In 2017, she received the Cedric Literary Award for poetry.

Chris Price was born in Reading, England, and moved with her family from England to Auckland, New Zealand, when she was four years old. She now lives in Wellington, New Zealand, and teaches creative writing full time at the International Institute of Modern Letters, Victoria University of Wellington. Her collections published by Auckland University Press are *Husk* (2002), *Brief Lives* (2006), *The Blind Singer* (2009), and *Beside Herself* (2016). She was an editor for Reed Publishing from 1989 until 1993 and the editor of *Landfall* from 1993 to 2000.

Jon Riccio is from Michigan, USA. He received his PhD from the University of Southern Mississippi's Center for Writers. Recent work appears in print or online at *The Cincinnati Review, COAST | NoCOAST,*

The Ekphrastic Review, E-ratio, Pouch, etc. He is the author of the full-length collection, *Agoreography (*3: A Taos Press, 2022) and two chapbooks entitled *Prodigal Cocktail Umbrella* (Trainwreck Press) and *Eye Romanov* (SurVision Books, 2021). He serves as a contributing interviewer for the University of Arizona Poetry Center's *1508* blog.

Matthew Rohrer lives in Brooklyn, New York and teaches creative writing at New York University. He is the author of 10 books of poems, most recently *The Sky Contains The Plans*, published by Wave Books. He was a co-founder of Fence Magazine and Fence Books, and his work has been widely anthologised. He has participated in residencies at MoMA and the Henry Art Gallery (Seattle). Awards include The Hopwood Award, a Pushcart Prize, the Believer Book Award, and a shortlist for the Griffin International Poetry Prize.

Jerome Rothenberg was born and raised in New York City, and now lives in California. An internationally known poet, translator, performance artist, with over eighty books of poetry and essays, he is also an anthologist, whose anthologies include *Technicians of the Sacred*, *Shaking the Pumpkin*, and the three-volume *Poems for the Millennium*. He has been the recipient of many honors, including an American Book Award, two PEN Oakland Josephine Miles Literary Awards, and two PEN Center USA West Translation Awards.

Jake Sheff is a pediatrician and veteran of the US Air Force living in Oregon. His poems and short stories have been published widely. His full-length collection of formal poetry, "A Kiss to Betray the Universe," is available from White Violet Press. His chapbooks are *Looting Versailles* (Alabaster Leaves Publishing, 2013), and *The Rites of Tires* published by SurVision Books in 2022.

Julia Stakhivska was born in Zhytomyr, Ukraine, and now lives in Kyiv. She was trained as a visual artist before studying the Ukrainian language and literature at Ostroh Academy and at National University of Kyiv-Mohyla Academy. She has published three critically-acclaimed collections of poetry, *The Ovary of Thoughts* (2003), *Little Red Man* (2009) and *Verde* (2015), as well as her translations from Czesław Miłosz. English translations of her poems appear in *The Frontier*, an anthology of contemporary Ukrainian poetry in English translation (ed. by Anatoly Kudryavitsky; Glagoslav Publications, London, UK, 2017).

Thomas Townsley is from New Hartford, NY. He currently teaches in the Humanities Department at Mohawk Valley Community College. His collections of poetry are *Night Class for Insomniacs* (Black Rabbit Press, 2018), *Holding A Séance By Myself* (Standing Stone Books, 2020), and *I Pray This Letter Reaches You In Time* (Doubly Mad Books, 2022), as well as *Tangent of Ardency* (SurVision Books, 2020). His work appears in *The Decadent Review, Stone Canoe, SurVision, Doubly Mad*, etc.

Marc Vincenz lives on a farm in Western Massachusetts. A poet, fiction writer, translator, editor, musician and artist, he has published over 30 books of poetry, fiction and translation. His work appears in *The Nation, Ploughshares, Raritan, World Literature Today,* and *The Los Angeles Review of Books.* He is editor and publisher of MadHat Press, and publisher of New American Writing. His latest books are *There Might Be a Moon or a Dog* (Gazebo Books, Australia, 2022) and *The Pearl Diver of Irunmani* (White Pine Press, forthcoming 2023).

Les Wicks was born and grew up in western suburbs of Sydney, Australia. He obtained a Bachelor of Arts in History at Macquarie University, and later a degree in industrial law. He lived in Sydney and London, was one of the founders of the Poets' Union in New South Wales. He has published thirteen poetry collections, the latest being *Getting By Not Fitting In* (Island Press, Australia, 2016). He won the Struga Poetry Award in Macedonia (2014).

Joshua Marie Wilkinson lives in Seattle. He is the author of nine books of poetry, including *Selenography, Swamp Isthmus,* and *Meadow Slasher.*His work also appears in *Poetry, The Believer, Tin House, Pen America,* and a number of anthologies. Two new books are forthcoming in 2023: *Bad Woods,* the final volume of his *No Volta* pentalogy, will be available soon from Sidebrow; and Fonograf Editions will release his debut novel, *Trouble Finds You,* before the end of the year.

Jeffrey Cyphers Wright is a publisher, critic, eco-activist, impresario, puppeteer, and artist living in N.Y.C. He is author of 19 books of verse, including including *Blue Lyre* from Dos Madres Press, *Party Everywhere* from Xanadu, and *Doppelgängster* from MadHat Press. He is a recipient of the Kathy Acker Award for both writing and publishing. The former publisher of *Cover Magazine, The Underground National,* he now publishes *Live Mag!* His website is www.jeffreycypherswright.com.

Paloma Yannakakis is a Mexican-Greek-American poet who lives and teaches in New York. Her poems appear in *Lana Turner, Washington Square, Denver Quarterly, Bodega, Green Mountains Review, SurVision,* and *Afternoon Visitor.* She serves on the editorial board of *House Mountain Review.* Her chapbook is *Double Take* (Finishing Line Press, 2023).

John Yau was born in Lynn, Massachusetts, of Chinese-American parentage. He studied at Boston University, and received his BA from Bard College and his MFA from Brooklyn College. Yau was the arts editor of *The Brooklyn Rail* from 2006 to 2011. He currently teaches art criticism at Mason Gross School of the Arts and Rutgers University. Yau has published many collections of poetry, the latest being *Further Adventures in Monochrome* (Copper Canyon Press, 2012). His awards include the Lavan Award from the Academy of American Poets, the *American Poetry Review* Jerome Shestack Award, and a 1988 New York Foundation for the Arts Award. He resides in New York City.

Andrew Zawacki currently teaches at the University of Georgia, USA. He is the author of five books of poetry: *Unsun : f/11* (2019), *Videotape* (2013), *Petals of Zero Petals of One* (2009), *Anabranch* (2004), and *By Reason of Breakings* (2002). His many chapbooks include *Waterfall Plot* (2019), *Sonnensonnets* (2019), *Kaeshi-waza* (2018), *Arrow's shadow* (2017), *Georgia* (2013), and *Glassscape* (2011). He has also published four books in France: *Sonnetssonnants,* translated by Anne Portugal; *Georgia* and *Carnet Bartleby,* both translated by Sika Fakambi; and *Par Raison de brisants,* translated by Antoine Cazé and a finalist for the Prix Nelly Sachs. *Anabranche,* translated by Sika Fakambi, is forthcoming.

Selected Poetry Titles Published by SurVision Books

Order our books from http://survisionmagazine.com

Seeds of Gravity: An Anthology of Contemporary Surrealist Poetry from Ireland
Edited by Anatoly Kudryavitsky
ISBN 978-1-912963-18-8

Invasion: An Anthology of Ukrainian Poetry about the War
Edited by Tony Kitt
ISBN 978-1-912963-32-4

Noelle Kocot. *Humanity*
(New Poetics: USA)
ISBN 978-1-9995903-0-7

Marc Vincenz. *Einstein Fledermaus*
(New Poetics: USA)
ISBN 978-1-912963-20-1

Helen Ivory. *Maps of the Abandoned City*
(New Poetics: England)
ISBN 978-1-912963-04-1

Tony Kitt. *The Magic Phlute*
(New Poetics: Ireland)
ISBN 978-1-912963-08-9

Clayre Benzadón. *Liminal Zenith*
(New Poetics: USA)
ISBN 978-1-912963-11-9

Thomas Townsley. *Tangent of Ardency*
(New Poetics: USA)
ISBN 978-1-912963-15-7

Jake Sheff. *The Rites of Tires*
(New Poetics: USA)
ISBN 978-1-912963-37-9

Mikko Harvey & Jake Bauer. *Idaho Falls*
(Winner of James Tate Poetry Prize 2018)
ISBN 978-1-912963-02-7

John Bradley. *Spontaneous Mummification*
(Winner of James Tate Poetry Prize 2019)
ISBN 978-1-912963-13-3

John Thomas Allen. *Rolling in the Third Eye*
(Winner of James Tate Poetry Prize 2019)
ISBN 978-1-912963-15-7

Nicholas Alexander Hayes. *Amorphous Organics*
(Winner of James Tate Poetry Prize 2019)
ISBN 978-1-912963-10-2

Gary Glauber. *The Covalence of Equanimity*
(Winner of James Tate Poetry Prize 2019)
ISBN 978-1-912963-12-6

Charles Kell. *Pierre Mask*
(Winner of James Tate Poetry Prize 2019)
ISBN 978-1-912963-19-5

Alison Dunhill. *As Pure as Coal Dust*
(Winner of James Tate Poetry Prize 2020)
ISBN 978-1-912963-23-2

Jon Riccio. *Eye, Romanov*
(Winner of James Tate Poetry Prize 2020)
ISBN 978-1-912963-24-9

Charles Borkhuis. *Spontaneous Combustion*
(Winner of James Tate Poetry Prize 2021)
ISBN 978-1-912963-30-0

Noah Falck and Matt McBride. *Prerecorded Weather*
(Winner of James Tate Poetry Prize 2022)
ISBN 978-1-912963-39-3

Michael Zeferino Spring. *Kahlo's Window*
(Winner of James Tate Poetry Prize 2022)
ISBN 978-1-912963-40-9

Dominique Hecq. *Endgame with No Ending*
(Winner of James Tate Poetry Prize 2022)
ISBN 978-1-912963-42-3

Heikki Huotari. *To Justify the Butterfly*
(Winner of James Tate Poetry Prize 2022)
ISBN 978-1-912963-41-6

J V Birch. *ice cream 'n' tar*
(Winner of James Tate Poetry Prize 2022)
ISBN 978-1-912963-43-0

Oz Hardwick. *A Census of Preconceptions*
ISBN 978-1-912963-38-6

Ciaran O'Driscoll. *Angel Hour*
ISBN 978-1-912963-27-0

George Kalamaras. *That Moment of Wept*
ISBN 978-1-9995903-7-6

George Kalamaras. *Through the Silk-Heavy Rains*
ISBN 978-1-912963-28-7

www.ingramcontent.com/pod-product-compliance
Lightning Source LLC
Chambersburg PA
CBHW060529100426
42743CB00009B/1466